HOW TO WRITE BETTER MIDJOURNEY PROMPTS BY EXAMPLE

By

Dr. Hesham Mohamed Elsherif

ABOUT THE AUTHOR

Dr. Hesham Mohamed Elsherif stands at the forefront of library management and research, boasting an impressive 22-year tenure in the field. Holding dual doctoral degrees, one in Management and Organizational Leadership and the other in Information Systems and Technology, Dr. Elsherif brings a unique blend of knowledge to any intellectual endeavor. An expert in Empirical research methodology, Dr. Elsherif specializes particularly in the Qualitative approach and Action research. This specialization has not only strengthened his research endeavors but has also allowed him to contribute invaluable insights and advancements in these areas.

Over the years, Dr. Elsherif has made significant contributions to the academic world not only as a professional researcher but also as an Adjunct Professor. This multifaceted role in the educational landscape has further solidified his reputation as a thought leader and pioneer. Furthermore, Dr. Elsherif's expertise isn't confined to one region. He has served as a consultant to numerous educational institutions on an international scale, sharing best practices, innovative strategies, and his deep insights into the ever-evolving realms of management and technology.

Combining a passion for education with an unparalleled depth of knowledge, Dr. Elsherif continues to inspire, educate, and lead in both the library and academic communities.

PREFACE

The Art and Science of Writing Midjourney Prompts

In the ever-evolving landscape of artificial intelligence and digital art, Midjourney stands as a beacon of creativity and innovation. This AI-powered tool has revolutionized the way we generate and interact with visual content, opening doors to artistic expressions that were once beyond reach. Yet, like any powerful tool, its true potential is unlocked only through mastery and understanding. This book, "How to Write Better Midjourney Prompts," is your comprehensive guide to achieving that mastery.

Why This Book?

The ability to communicate effectively with AI is becoming an essential skill in various fields, from digital marketing to entertainment and beyond. Midjourney, with its sophisticated algorithms, requires precise and thoughtful input to produce the best results. Writing effective prompts is both an art and a science, requiring a blend of creativity, clarity, and technical knowledge. This book aims to demystify the process, providing you with the tools and techniques needed to harness the full power of Midjourney.

A Journey of Discovery

When I first encountered Midjourney, I was both amazed and intrigued by its capabilities. The images it generated were stunning, yet I quickly realized that the quality of the output was directly tied to the quality of the input. Simple prompts yielded simple results, while detailed and imaginative prompts brought forth extraordinary creations. This realization sparked a journey of discovery, experimentation, and learning that I am excited to share with you.

What You Will Learn

This book is structured to take you from the basics of prompt writing to advanced techniques that will enable you to create sophisticated and nuanced images. Each chapter builds on the last, gradually introducing more complex concepts and strategies. You will learn how to:

- Craft detailed and specific prompts that guide Midjourney effectively.

- Utilize key parameters to fine-tune your results.

- Experiment with synonyms and varied vocabulary to enhance creativity.

- Employ positive language to avoid common pitfalls.

- Embrace ambiguity and randomness for unique and unexpected outcomes.

- Iterate and refine your prompts for continuous improvement.

- Break down complex images into multi-prompts for greater detail and accuracy.

Practical Insights and Real-World Applications

Throughout the book, you will find practical exercises, real-world case studies, and expert tips that provide deeper insights into effective prompt writing. These elements are designed to help you apply the concepts in real-time, transforming theoretical knowledge into practical skills. Whether you are a digital artist, a content creator, or simply someone passionate about AI, this book offers valuable guidance to elevate your work with Midjourney.

The Future of AI and Creativity

As we look to the future, the role of AI in creativity and artistic expression will only continue to grow. Understanding how to interact with these technologies will be crucial for anyone looking to stay ahead in the creative industries. This book is not just about writing better prompts; it's about embracing the future of art and technology, and positioning yourself at the forefront of this exciting evolution.

Let's Begin

As you embark on this journey, remember that learning to write effective Midjourney prompts is a process of continuous exploration and experimentation. I encourage you to be bold, to try new things, and to embrace the unexpected. The pages that follow are filled with knowledge, but the true magic happens when you apply that knowledge and watch your creative visions come to life.

Welcome to the world of Midjourney. Let's create something extraordinary together.

Dr. Hesham Mohamed Elsherif

Table of Contents

Introduction

<u>What is Midjourney?</u>

Midjourney represents a significant leap forward in the realm of AI-driven creativity. It is an advanced AI tool designed to generate high-quality images based on textual descriptions provided by users. As part of a broader movement towards integrating artificial intelligence with creative processes, Midjourney exemplifies how technology can enhance and expand human artistic capabilities.

Origins and Development

Midjourney was developed by a team of experts in artificial intelligence, computer graphics, and digital art. The goal was to create a tool that could interpret textual prompts and convert them into visually stunning images, thereby bridging the gap between verbal and visual creativity. The technology behind Midjourney leverages sophisticated machine learning algorithms and vast datasets of images to understand and replicate a wide range of artistic styles and subjects.

How Midjourney Works

At its core, Midjourney uses a type of machine learning model known as a Generative Adversarial Network (GAN). GANs consist of two neural networks, the generator and the discriminator, that work in tandem to produce realistic images. The generator creates images based on the input it receives, while the discriminator evaluates these images against real-world examples, providing feedback to the generator to improve its output.

When a user inputs a text prompt, Midjourney processes the language through a natural language processing (NLP) system to understand the context and specifics of the request. This processed data is then fed into the GAN, which generates an image that best matches the description provided.

Key Features of Midjourney

1. **Text-to-Image Conversion**: Midjourney's primary function is to convert textual descriptions into images. This allows users to describe their vision in words and see it materialize visually.

2. **Style Adaptation**: The tool can adapt to a wide variety of artistic styles, from photorealistic images to abstract art, depending on the user's specifications. This versatility makes it a valuable resource for artists, designers, and creatives across different fields.

3. **Parameter Customization**: Users can fine-tune their results using various parameters such as aspect ratio, chaos, and stylize. This customization ensures that the generated images closely align with the user's creative vision.

4. **Iterative Improvement**: Midjourney supports iterative refinement, allowing users to tweak their prompts and generate improved versions of their images. This process of continuous feedback and adjustment helps achieve the desired result more efficiently.

Applications of Midjourney

Midjourney has found applications in numerous fields, reflecting its versatility and power:

- **Digital Art and Illustration**: Artists use Midjourney to explore new styles, generate inspiration, and create unique pieces of digital art.

- **Marketing and Advertising**: Marketers leverage Midjourney to create engaging visuals for campaigns, social media, and branding materials.

- **Content Creation**: Writers and content creators utilize Midjourney to produce illustrations that complement their stories and articles.

- **Education**: Educators employ Midjourney to generate visual aids and materials that enhance the learning experience.

The Impact of Midjourney on Creativity

Midjourney is more than just a tool; it represents a paradigm shift in how we approach creativity and artistic production. By democratizing access to high-quality image generation, it empowers individuals and small businesses to compete with larger entities in terms of visual content creation. Moreover, it fosters a new form of collaboration between humans and machines, where AI acts as a co-creator, amplifying human creativity rather than replacing it.

Looking Ahead

The development and continuous improvement of Midjourney signal exciting times for the future of AI in art. As the technology evolves, we can expect even more sophisticated capabilities, broader applications, and deeper integration with various creative processes. Embracing tools like Midjourney will be crucial for staying ahead in the rapidly changing landscape of digital creativity.

In the chapters that follow, we will delve deeper into the intricacies of writing effective prompts for Midjourney, exploring techniques and strategies to maximize the tool's potential and unlock your creative prowess.

Importance of Effective Prompts

The Role of Prompts in AI-Generated Art

In the realm of AI-generated art, the quality of the output is intrinsically linked to the quality of the input. Midjourney, like many other AI art tools, relies heavily on the prompts provided by users to create images that meet their expectations. Effective prompts are crucial because they serve as the blueprint for the AI's creative process, guiding it in the generation of visually appealing and conceptually accurate images. A well-crafted prompt can mean the difference between an image that aligns perfectly with your vision and one that falls short.

Enhancing Creativity and Precision

One of the primary reasons effective prompts are so important is that they enhance both creativity and precision in the generated images. By providing clear, detailed, and imaginative prompts, users can tap into the AI's full potential, exploring a wide range of artistic styles and subjects. Detailed prompts help the AI understand the nuances of the user's vision, leading to more accurate and satisfying results.

Avoiding Common Pitfalls

Poorly constructed prompts can lead to ambiguous or unintended results, wasting both time and resources. Common pitfalls in prompt writing include vagueness, lack of detail, and the use of negative language. For example, a prompt like "a dog" is too vague and can result in a wide variety of interpretations, whereas "a golden retriever playing fetch in a sunny park" provides specific details that guide the AI more effectively.

Leveraging AI Capabilities

Effective prompts also allow users to leverage the full capabilities of Midjourney. By understanding and utilizing the various parameters and customization options available, users can fine-tune their prompts to achieve the desired artistic effects. Parameters such as aspect ratio, chaos, and stylize can be used to control the composition, variability, and style of the generated images, ensuring that the output matches the user's creative vision.

Facilitating Iteration and Improvement

Another critical aspect of effective prompt writing is its role in facilitating iteration and improvement. AI-generated art is often an iterative process, where users refine their prompts based on the results to achieve better outcomes. Clear and detailed prompts provide a solid foundation for this iterative process, making it easier to identify what needs to be adjusted and how to guide the AI towards the desired result.

Enabling Complex Creations

For more complex and detailed images, effective prompts are essential. Multi-prompt techniques, where a complex image is broken down into several simpler prompts, can be particularly useful. This approach allows users to manage the complexity of the image creation process, ensuring that each element is accurately represented and harmoniously integrated into the final composition

Encouraging Experimentation and Innovation

Well-crafted prompts encourage users to experiment and innovate, pushing the boundaries of what AI-generated art can achieve. By playing with different styles, subjects, and parameters, users can discover new creative possibilities and produce unique and compelling images. This spirit of experimentation is at the heart of the artistic process, and effective prompts are the key to unlocking it.

The importance of effective prompts in AI-generated art cannot be overstated. They are the cornerstone of the creative process, providing the necessary guidance for the AI to produce high-quality, accurate, and visually appealing images. By mastering the art of prompt writing, users can fully harness the power of Midjourney, transforming their creative visions into reality and exploring the limitless possibilities of AI-enhanced artistry. The chapters that follow will delve deeper into the techniques and strategies for crafting effective prompts, equipping you with the skills needed to excel in this exciting field.

Chapter 1: Understanding Midjourney

The Evolution of AI Art Generation

The Genesis of AI Art

Artificial intelligence has long been a subject of fascination and speculation, with its roots tracing back to the mid-20th century. Initially, AI research focused on logical reasoning, problem-solving, and knowledge representation. However, the advent of machine learning and neural networks in the 1980s and 1990s marked a pivotal shift towards more sophisticated and adaptive AI systems. These advancements laid the groundwork for AI applications in various fields, including art.

Early Experiments and Milestones

The early 2000s saw the first significant attempts to blend AI with artistic creation. These experiments primarily involved rule-based systems and basic neural networks to generate rudimentary images and music. Although these early efforts were limited in complexity and creativity, they demonstrated the potential for AI to contribute to artistic processes.

One notable milestone was the development of Generative Adversarial Networks (GANs) by Ian Goodfellow and his colleagues in 2014. GANs consist of two neural networks: a generator that creates images and a discriminator that evaluates their realism. This adversarial process significantly improved the quality of AI-generated images, making them more realistic and detailed.

The Rise of AI-Generated Art

The mid-2010s marked a significant leap in AI art generation, with advancements in deep learning and computational power enabling more complex and creative outputs. Several AI art tools and platforms emerged during this period, showcasing the growing capabilities of AI in generating high-quality visual content.

DeepArt and Style Transfer: DeepArt and other style transfer algorithms allowed users to apply the stylistic elements of one image to another. By training neural networks on famous artworks, these algorithms could transform ordinary photos into pieces resembling the styles of Van Gogh, Picasso, and other renowned artists. This technology highlighted AI's ability to blend different artistic styles seamlessly.

Google DeepDream: Google's DeepDream, introduced in 2015, pushed the boundaries of AI creativity by visualizing the patterns learned by neural networks. DeepDream's trippy and surreal images captured the public's imagination and demonstrated the potential for AI to create entirely new and abstract forms of art.

The Advent of Midjourney

Midjourney represents a culmination of these advancements, incorporating state-of-the-art AI techniques to deliver a powerful tool for generating high-quality images from textual descriptions. By leveraging sophisticated machine learning algorithms and extensive datasets, Midjourney can interpret and visualize user prompts with remarkable accuracy and creativity.

Key Innovations in Midjourney

Text-to-Image Synthesis: Midjourney excels in converting textual descriptions into detailed and visually appealing images. This capability is built on advanced natural language processing (NLP) techniques that allow the AI to understand the nuances and specifics of user inputs.

Generative Adversarial Networks (GANs): Midjourney utilizes GANs to enhance the realism and quality of generated images. The interplay between the generator and discriminator ensures continuous improvement, producing images that are both creative and lifelike.

Customization and Parameters: One of Midjourney's standout features is its extensive customization options. Users can adjust parameters such as aspect ratio, chaos, and stylize to fine-tune the generated images according to their creative vision. This level of control allows for precise and personalized outputs.

Iterative Refinement: Midjourney supports an iterative approach to image generation. Users can refine their prompts and regenerate images, allowing for continuous improvement and experimentation. This feature is particularly valuable for complex and detailed projects.

The Impact of Midjourney on the Art World

Midjourney and similar AI art tools have significantly impacted the art world by democratizing access to high-quality image generation. Artists, designers, marketers, and educators can now leverage AI to enhance their creative processes, explore new styles, and produce unique visual content.

The ability to quickly and efficiently generate high-quality images has also transformed industries such as marketing and advertising, where visual content plays a crucial role. Midjourney's versatility and ease of use make it a valuable asset for professionals and hobbyists alike.

The Future of AI Art Generation

The evolution of AI art generation is far from over. As technology continues to advance, we can expect even more sophisticated and capable AI tools. Future developments may include:

- **Enhanced Realism and Detail**: Continued improvements in GANs and other AI models will likely lead to even more realistic and detailed images.

- **Greater Creative Collaboration**: AI tools will increasingly become collaborators in the creative process, offering suggestions and enhancements that complement human creativity.

- **Broader Applications**: AI-generated art will find applications in new fields, from virtual reality and gaming to architecture and fashion design.

The journey of AI art generation has been marked by significant milestones and continuous innovation. From early experiments to the sophisticated capabilities of Midjourney, AI has proven to be a powerful ally in the realm of creativity. As we look to the future, the potential for AI to further revolutionize art and design is limitless, offering exciting possibilities for artists and creators worldwide.

How Midjourney Works

The Core Technology

Midjourney is built on advanced artificial intelligence technologies that enable it to generate high-quality images from textual descriptions. The core technology driving Midjourney is a combination of natural language processing (NLP) and generative adversarial networks (GANs), which work together to interpret and visualize user prompts.

Natural Language Processing (NLP)

Natural Language Processing (NLP) is a branch of artificial intelligence that focuses on the interaction between computers and humans through natural language. NLP enables Midjourney to understand and process the textual prompts provided by users. Here's how it works:

1. **Text Parsing**:

o   When a user inputs a text prompt, Midjourney first parses the text to understand its structure and meaning. This involves breaking down the text into its constituent parts, such as nouns, verbs, adjectives, and adverbs.

2. **Semantic Analysis**:

o   After parsing the text, Midjourney performs semantic analysis to understand the context and relationships between different elements in the prompt. This step is crucial for accurately interpreting the user's intent and ensuring that the generated image aligns with the description.

3. **Contextual Understanding**:

o   NLP allows Midjourney to grasp the nuances and subtleties of the text. For instance, understanding that "a cat sitting on a windowsill" involves not just the cat and the windowsill, but also the positional relationship between them. This level of contextual understanding ensures more accurate and relevant image generation.

Generative Adversarial Networks (GANs)

Generative Adversarial Networks (GANs) are a class of machine learning frameworks designed to generate realistic data. A GAN consists of two neural networks: the generator and the discriminator. These networks work in tandem to produce high-quality images:

1. **The Generator**:

   o   The generator creates images based on the input it receives from the NLP system. Its goal is to produce images that are as realistic and accurate as possible, according to the textual description.

2. **The Discriminator**:

   o   The discriminator's role is to evaluate the images generated by the generator. It compares these images to real-world examples, providing feedback on their realism and quality.

3. **Adversarial Training**:

   o   The generator and discriminator are trained together in a process known as adversarial training. The generator tries to create convincing images, while the discriminator works to distinguish between real and generated images. This adversarial process continues until the generator produces images that are indistinguishable from real ones.

The Process of Image Generation

The process of generating images in Midjourney involves several key steps:

1. **Input Processing**:

o The user provides a textual description of the desired image. This text is processed by the NLP system, which extracts meaningful features and context.

2. **Feature Extraction**:

o The extracted features are then used by the generator to create an initial image. This image is a rough representation based on the input text.

3. **Image Refinement**:

o The initial image is evaluated by the discriminator, which provides feedback to the generator. Based on this feedback, the generator refines the image, making it more detailed and realistic.

4. **Iterative Improvement**:

o This process of generation and evaluation continues iteratively. Each iteration results in a more refined image, with the generator constantly improving its output based on the discriminator's feedback.

5. **Final Output**:

o Once the image reaches a satisfactory level of quality and accuracy, it is presented to the user as the final output.

Customization and Parameters

Midjourney allows users to customize their image generation process through various parameters. These parameters provide greater control over the final output:

1. **Aspect Ratio**:

o   Users can specify the aspect ratio of the image, such as 16:9 or 4:3, to fit their specific needs.

2. **Chaos**:

o   The chaos parameter adjusts the level of randomness and variation in the generated images. Higher chaos values lead to more diverse and experimental outputs.

3. **Stylize**:

o   The stylize parameter influences the artistic style applied to the image. Users can choose from a range of styles, from photorealistic to abstract.

Iterative Refinement and User Feedback

One of the strengths of Midjourney is its support for iterative refinement. Users can provide feedback on the generated images and adjust their prompts to achieve better results. This iterative process allows for continuous improvement and ensures that the final output closely matches the user's creative vision.

Understanding how Midjourney works provides valuable insights into its capabilities and potential. By leveraging advanced NLP and GAN technologies, Midjourney can interpret complex textual descriptions and generate high-quality images that reflect the user's intent. The ability to customize and iteratively refine outputs makes Midjourney a powerful tool for artists, designers, and anyone looking to explore the creative possibilities of AI-generated art.

Key Differences Between Midjourney and Other AI Tools

Introduction to AI Art Tools

Artificial Intelligence (AI) has revolutionized various fields, including art. Numerous AI tools are available for generating images, each with unique features and capabilities. Understanding the key differences between Midjourney and other AI art tools can help users select the best tool for their specific needs.

1. Text-to-Image Synthesis

Midjourney:

- Midjourney excels at converting textual descriptions into high-quality images. Its advanced Natural Language Processing (NLP) capabilities allow it to understand complex prompts and generate images that closely match the user's intent. This makes Midjourney particularly effective for users who want to articulate detailed and nuanced artistic visions through text.

Other AI Tools:

- While other AI tools like DALL-E and CLIP also offer text-to-image synthesis, they may not always match the level of detail and contextual understanding provided by Midjourney. Some tools might excel in specific styles or contexts but lack the versatility that Midjourney offers in interpreting a wide range of descriptions.

2. Customization and Control

Midjourney:

- Midjourney offers extensive customization options, allowing users to fine-tune various parameters such as aspect ratio, chaos, and stylize. This level of control enables users to precisely shape the output according to their creative vision, making Midjourney highly versatile and adaptable.

Other AI Tools:

- Many AI art tools provide customization features, but the extent and ease of use can vary. Tools like Artbreeder allow users to mix and modify images but might not offer the same depth of textual prompt customization as Midjourney. Some tools might focus more on pre-defined styles and templates, limiting user control over the final output.

3. Iterative Refinement

Midjourney:

- A standout feature of Midjourney is its support for iterative refinement. Users can tweak their prompts and regenerate images to achieve better results. This iterative process allows for continuous improvement, ensuring that the final output aligns closely with the user's creative vision.

Other AI Tools:

- While iterative refinement is available in some AI tools, it is not always as intuitive or integrated as in Midjourney. For instance, tools like Runway ML and DeepArt offer iteration capabilities but may require more manual intervention or lack the seamless feedback loop that Midjourney provides.

4. Artistic Style Adaptation

Midjourney:

- Midjourney can adapt to a wide array of artistic styles, from photorealistic to abstract. This flexibility makes it suitable for various artistic projects, whether users seek realistic portraits, fantastical landscapes, or avant-garde designs.

Other AI Tools:

- Tools like DeepArt and Prisma are renowned for their style transfer capabilities, allowing users to apply specific artistic styles to images. However, they may not offer the same breadth of style adaptation or the ability to generate entirely new images based on text descriptions, as Midjourney does.

5. Community and Support

Midjourney:

- Midjourney has a strong community and support system, providing users with resources, tutorials, and forums to share their experiences and get help. This community-driven approach fosters collaboration and learning, enhancing the overall user experience.

Other AI Tools:

- Other AI tools also have active communities and support systems, but the extent and accessibility can vary. Platforms like Artbreeder and DALL-E have substantial user bases, yet the level of direct support and the richness of community interactions might differ compared to Midjourney.

6. User Experience and Interface

Midjourney:

- Midjourney is designed with user experience in mind, offering an intuitive interface that simplifies the process of generating and refining images. The focus on usability makes it accessible to both beginners and experienced users.

Other AI Tools:

- The user experience can vary widely among other AI tools. Some, like Runway ML, offer professional-grade interfaces with extensive features, which might be overwhelming for beginners. Others, like Prisma, provide user-friendly mobile apps but may lack advanced customization options.

Conclusion

Midjourney distinguishes itself from other AI art tools through its advanced text-to-image synthesis, extensive customization options, iterative refinement capabilities, and versatile style adaptation. These features, combined with a strong community and user-friendly interface, make Midjourney a powerful tool for artists, designers, and anyone looking to explore the creative possibilities of AI-generated art. By understanding these key differences, users can make informed decisions about which AI tool best suits their needs and artistic goals.

Chapter 2: Fundamentals of Prompt Writing

Introduction to Prompt Writing

Writing effective prompts is essential for harnessing the full potential of AI tools like Midjourney. Prompts are the instructions that guide the AI in generating images, and their quality directly influences the output.

Basic Structure of a Prompt

A well-structured prompt consists of several key components that collectively provide clear and detailed instructions to the AI. These components include:

1. **Subject**:

   o The main focus of the image. This could be a person, animal, object, or scene. For example, "a cat," "a mountain," or "a person reading a book."

2. **Action**:

   o What the subject is doing. Actions help to add dynamism and context to the image. For instance, "a cat sleeping," "a mountain under the sunset," or "a person reading a book in a library."

3. **Context and Setting**:

   o The environment or background where the subject is located. This provides additional details that enrich the image. Examples include "a cat sleeping on a windowsill," "a mountain under the sunset in a serene valley," or "a person reading a book in a quiet library."

4. **Attributes and Descriptors**:

o   Descriptive words that add more detail about the subject, action, and setting. These can include colors, emotions, styles, and other specific attributes. For example, "a fluffy white cat sleeping on a sunny windowsill," "a majestic mountain under the golden sunset in a serene valley," or "a young woman with glasses reading a thick novel in a quiet, dimly lit library."

The Importance of Clarity and Specificity

Clarity and specificity are crucial in prompt writing because they reduce ambiguity and ensure that the AI generates images that closely match your vision. Here's how to achieve clarity and specificity:

1. **Use Descriptive Language**:

o   The more detailed and vivid your descriptions, the better the AI can visualize your request. Instead of saying "a tree," specify "a tall oak tree with lush green leaves."

2. **Be Specific with Actions**:

o   Clearly define what the subject is doing. For example, rather than "a person," describe "a person jogging along a beach at sunrise."

3. **Provide Context**:

o   Include relevant background details to set the scene. For example, "a cat sleeping" becomes more vivid as "a fluffy white cat sleeping on a sunny windowsill in a cozy living room."

4. **Avoid Ambiguity**:

o   Ambiguous terms can lead to unexpected results. Ensure your prompt is precise. For example, "an old building" could be more specifically described as "a 19th-century Gothic-style building with ivy-covered walls."

Common Mistakes to Avoid

Avoiding common pitfalls in prompt writing can significantly improve the quality of the generated images. Here are some mistakes to watch out for:

1. **Vagueness**:

- Vague prompts lead to unpredictable results. Instead of "a beautiful scene," specify what makes the scene beautiful, such as "a serene lake surrounded by blooming cherry blossoms under a clear blue sky."

2. **Overcomplication**:

- While details are important, overly complex prompts can confuse the AI. Break down complex scenes into simpler elements. For example, instead of "a bustling cityscape with people, cars, buildings, and advertisements," you might specify "a busy street in New York City with yellow taxis, skyscrapers, and digital billboards."

3. **Negative Language**:

- Negative terms can be misinterpreted by the AI. Instead of "a room without windows," describe "a windowless room."

4. **Inconsistent Details**:

- Ensure that all parts of your prompt are consistent and coherent. Avoid conflicting descriptions, such as "a sunny night" or "a quiet bustling market."

Examples of Effective Prompts

To illustrate these principles, here are some examples of effective prompts compared to less effective ones:

- **Less Effective**: "A dog"

  o **More Effective**: "A golden retriever puppy playing with a red ball in a grassy backyard on a sunny day"

- **Less Effective**: "A city"

  o **More Effective**: "A vibrant cityscape of Tokyo at night, with neon signs, bustling streets, and cherry blossom trees in the background"

- **Less Effective**: "A person"

  o **More Effective**: "A young woman with curly brown hair and glasses, sitting at a wooden desk, typing on a laptop in a cozy, book-filled study"

Practical Tips for Writing Prompts

1. **Start Simple**:

   o Begin with a basic idea and gradually add details. This approach helps in building a clear and concise prompt.

2. **Iterate and Refine**:

   o Don't hesitate to refine your prompts based on the results you get. Iteration helps in honing the accuracy and quality of the output.

3. **Use Positive Descriptions**:

   o Frame your prompts positively. Instead of "not dark," use "brightly lit."

4. **Practice and Experiment**:

o Practice writing prompts regularly and experiment with different styles and levels of detail to understand what works best.

Basic Structure of a Prompt

Writing effective prompts for Midjourney is akin to providing detailed instructions to an artist. The clearer and more specific your instructions, the better the resulting artwork will align with your vision. A well-structured prompt consists of several key components: the subject, action, context and setting, and attributes and descriptors. Understanding and utilizing these components effectively will enhance the quality of the images generated.

Subject

The subject is the main focus of your image. It defines what or who the image is about. The subject can be a person, an animal, an object, or a scene. Clear identification of the subject is crucial for setting the foundation of your prompt.

Examples:

- **Person**: "a young woman"

- **Animal**: "a golden retriever"

- **Object**: "an ancient book"

- **Scene**: "a bustling market"

Action

The action describes what the subject is doing. It adds dynamism and context to the image, providing a narrative or activity that the subject is engaged in. This component is essential for giving life and movement to your image.

Examples:

- **Person**: "a young woman reading a book"

- **Animal**: "a golden retriever playing fetch"

- **Object**: "an ancient book lying open on a table"

- **Scene**: "a bustling market with vendors selling fruits and vegetables"

Context and Setting

The context and setting provide the environment or background for the subject and action. This element enriches the image by situating the subject within a specific place or situation, adding layers of detail that enhance the visual narrative.

Examples:

- **Person**: "a young woman reading a book in a cozy café"

- **Animal**: "a golden retriever playing fetch in a sunlit park"

- **Object**: "an ancient book lying open on a wooden table in a dimly lit library"

- **Scene**: "a bustling market with vendors selling fruits and vegetables in a quaint village square"

Attributes and Descriptors

Attributes and descriptors are detailed characteristics that provide additional information about the subject, action, and setting. They include visual details, emotional tones, and stylistic elements that further refine the image.

Examples:

- **Person**: "a young woman with curly brown hair and glasses, reading a book in a cozy, dimly lit café"

- **Animal**: "a golden retriever with a shiny coat, joyfully playing fetch in a sunlit, grassy park"

- **Object**: "an ancient book with weathered pages and a leather cover, lying open on a wooden table in a dimly lit, old library"

- **Scene**: "a bustling market with cheerful vendors selling vibrant fruits and vegetables in a quaint village square, under a clear blue sky"

Combining the Elements

Combining these elements effectively creates a comprehensive and vivid prompt that guides the AI to generate detailed and accurate images. Here's how a well-structured prompt integrates all components:

Example: "A young woman with curly brown hair and glasses, reading a thick novel in a cozy, dimly lit café, with a steaming cup of coffee on the table beside her."

In this example:

- **Subject**: "a young woman"

- **Action**: "reading a thick novel"

- **Context and Setting**: "in a cozy, dimly lit café"

- **Attributes and Descriptors**: "with curly brown hair and glasses" and "a steaming cup of coffee on the table beside her"

Practical Tips for Writing Effective Prompts

1. **Start with a Clear Idea**:

o   Begin with a clear concept of what you want the image to depict. Identify the subject, action, and setting in your mind before you start writing the prompt.

2. **Use Detailed Descriptions**:

o   The more details you provide, the more accurate and vivid the generated image will be. Include specific attributes and descriptors that paint a complete picture.

3. **Be Specific and Avoid Ambiguity**:

o   Specificity reduces the chances of misinterpretation. Avoid vague terms and be precise in your descriptions.

4. **Iterate and Refine**:

o   Don't hesitate to refine your prompts based on the results you get. Iterative improvements help in honing the accuracy and quality of the output.

5. **Balance Detail with Clarity**:

o   While details are important, ensure your prompt remains clear and easy to understand. Overloading with too many details can sometimes confuse the AI.

Mastering the basic structure of a prompt is the first step towards achieving high-quality AI-generated images. By focusing on the key components—subject, action, context and setting, and attributes and descriptors—you can craft detailed and vivid prompts that guide the AI effectively. This foundation will enable you to explore more advanced techniques and strategies, further enhancing your ability to create stunning visual content with Midjourney.

The Importance of Clarity and Specificity

Clarity and specificity are crucial elements in writing effective prompts for Midjourney. These elements help ensure that the AI accurately interprets and generates images that align closely with your creative vision. A clear and specific prompt minimizes ambiguity, reduces the potential for misinterpretation, and enhances the overall quality of the generated image.

Why Clarity and Specificity Matter

1. **Reducing Ambiguity**:

   o Ambiguous prompts can lead to unpredictable results. When a prompt is unclear, the AI might produce an image that does not match your expectations. By being clear and specific, you provide the AI with precise instructions, which helps in generating the desired output.

2. **Enhancing Detail**:

   o Detailed prompts allow the AI to incorporate specific elements and nuances into the image. The more detailed and vivid your descriptions, the richer and more accurate the generated image will be.

3. **Improving Accuracy**:

   o Clear and specific prompts improve the accuracy of the generated images. When the AI understands exactly what you want, it can create images that are closely aligned with your vision, reducing the need for multiple iterations and refinements.

Examples of Effective Prompts

Vague vs. Clear and Specific Prompts:

1. **Example 1: Describing a Person**

o **Vague**: "A man"

o **Clear and Specific**: "A tall man with short brown hair, wearing a blue suit and red tie, standing in front of a skyscraper"

o **Explanation**: The vague prompt "a man" provides minimal information, leading to a wide range of possible images. The specific prompt details the man's appearance, attire, and setting, guiding the AI to produce a precise image.

2. **Example 2: Describing a Scene**

o **Vague**: "A beach"

o **Clear and Specific**: "A serene beach at sunset, with golden sand, gentle waves, and a palm tree swaying in the breeze"

o **Explanation**: "A beach" is too general and could result in any number of beach scenes. The detailed prompt specifies the time of day, environmental elements, and mood, creating a clear picture for the AI to generate.

3. **Example 3: Describing an Object**

o **Vague**: "A car"

o **Clear and Specific**: "A vintage red convertible with white leather seats, parked on a cobblestone street under a clear blue sky"

o **Explanation**: The vague prompt "a car" could produce any type of car. The specific prompt includes details about the car's model, color, and setting, ensuring a more accurate and detailed image.

Practical Tips for Writing Clear and Specific Prompts

1. **Use Descriptive Language**:

   o   Incorporate adjectives and adverbs to provide detailed descriptions. For example, instead of "a dog," describe "a playful golden retriever puppy with a shiny coat."

2. **Specify Actions and Context**:

   o   Clearly define what the subject is doing and where the action is taking place. For instance, rather than "a person running," specify "a young woman jogging along a forest trail during autumn."

3. **Include Relevant Details**:

   o   Add details that contribute to the overall image. Mention colors, textures, emotions, and other attributes that help create a vivid picture. For example, instead of "a house," describe "a cozy cottage with a thatched roof, surrounded by blooming flowers and a white picket fence."

4. **Avoid Ambiguous Terms**:

   o   Steer clear of vague terms that can be interpreted in multiple ways. Instead of "a beautiful scene," describe what makes the scene beautiful, such as "a tranquil lake reflecting the golden hues of a setting sun, with mountains in the background."

5. **Break Down Complex Descriptions**:

   o   For intricate scenes, break down the description into manageable parts. Describe each element separately and then combine them into a cohesive prompt. For example, "a bustling marketplace" could be broken down into "vendors selling colorful fruits and vegetables," "shoppers browsing stalls," and "children playing near a fountain."

Clarity and specificity are essential for writing effective prompts that guide AI tools like Midjourney to generate high-quality images. By using descriptive language, specifying actions and contexts, including relevant details, avoiding ambiguity, and breaking down complex descriptions, you can create prompts that produce accurate and visually appealing results. Mastering these techniques will significantly enhance your ability to communicate with AI and realize your creative visions.

Common Mistakes to Avoid

Writing effective prompts for Midjourney requires attention to detail and an understanding of common pitfalls that can undermine the quality of the generated images. By recognizing and avoiding these mistakes, you can improve the accuracy and relevance of the AI-generated content.

Common Mistakes and How to Avoid Them

1. Vagueness

Mistake: Providing a prompt that is too vague, which leads to ambiguous and unpredictable results.

Example:

- **Vague**: "A car"

- **Specific**: "A vintage red convertible with white leather seats, parked on a cobblestone street under a clear blue sky"

Solution: Include specific details about the subject, such as color, type, and context. This helps the AI generate an image that closely matches your vision.

2. Overcomplication

Mistake: Including too many details in a single prompt, which can confuse the AI and result in a cluttered or incoherent image.

Example:

- **Overcomplicated**: "A bustling city street with cars, people, buildings, streetlights, billboards, shops, trees, and a fountain"

- **Simplified**: "A bustling city street with yellow taxis and people walking on the sidewalks"

Solution: Focus on the key elements that define the scene. If necessary, break down the description into multiple prompts or iterations to achieve the desired level of detail without overwhelming the AI.

3. **Negative Language**

Mistake: Using negative terms to describe what should be excluded, which can lead to confusion and unintended results.

Example:

- **Negative**: "A room without windows"

- **Positive**: "A windowless room"

Solution: Frame your prompts positively by describing what should be included rather than what should be excluded. This ensures clearer communication with the AI.

4. **Inconsistent Details**

Mistake: Including contradictory or inconsistent details that can confuse the AI and result in unrealistic or mismatched images.

Example:

- **Inconsistent**: "A sunny night scene"

- **Consistent**: "A starry night scene with a bright moon illuminating the landscape"

Solution: Ensure all details in the prompt are consistent and logically coherent. Double-check for any contradictions that might confuse the AI.

5. Overly General Terms

Mistake: Using general terms that do not provide enough guidance for the AI to generate a specific and accurate image.

Example:

- **General**: "A beautiful scene"

- **Specific**: "A tranquil beach at sunset with golden sand and gentle waves"

Solution: Use descriptive and specific language to convey a clear vision of the desired image. Focus on the characteristics that define what makes the scene beautiful or unique.

6. Ignoring Context

Mistake: Failing to provide context or background information, which can result in images that lack depth and relevance.

Example:

- **Without Context**: "A tree"

- **With Context**: "A tall oak tree with lush green leaves in a peaceful forest clearing"

Solution: Include context and setting to enrich the image and provide a more comprehensive visual narrative.

Practical Tips for Avoiding Common Mistakes

1. **Be Clear and Concise**:

o Aim for clarity and brevity in your prompts. Provide enough detail to guide the AI but avoid unnecessary complexity.

2. **Focus on Key Elements**:

o Identify the most important aspects of your image and emphasize them. This helps the AI prioritize the key elements that define the scene.

3. **Use Positive Descriptions**:

o Frame your prompts in a positive manner, describing what should be included rather than what should be excluded.

4. **Ensure Consistency**:

o Check for any contradictory or inconsistent details in your prompt. Make sure all elements work together logically and cohesively.

5. **Iterate and Refine**:

o Don't hesitate to refine your prompts based on the results. Iterative improvements help in honing the accuracy and quality of the generated images.

Avoiding common mistakes in prompt writing is crucial for achieving high-quality AI-generated images. By focusing on clarity, specificity, positive language, consistency, and context, you can guide Midjourney more effectively and realize your creative visions with greater accuracy. Mastering these fundamentals will significantly enhance your ability to communicate with AI and produce stunning visual content.

Conclusion

Mastering the fundamentals of prompt writing is essential for achieving the best results with Midjourney. By focusing on clarity, specificity, and detailed descriptions, and by avoiding common pitfalls, you can guide the AI to generate images that closely match your creative vision. In the next chapters, we will delve deeper into advanced techniques and strategies to further enhance your prompt writing skills, enabling you to fully harness the power of Midjourney.

Chapter 3: Detailed Descriptions

Detailed descriptions are the cornerstone of effective prompt writing for AI tools like Midjourney. They enable the AI to generate images that closely align with your vision by providing precise and vivid information about the subject, action, setting, and attributes. Detailed prompts help reduce ambiguity and ensure the AI captures the nuances of your creative intent.

The Importance of Detailed Descriptions

1. **Enhancing Accuracy**:

o   Detailed descriptions ensure that the AI understands exactly what you want, resulting in images that are more accurate and aligned with your vision.

2. **Adding Depth and Nuance**:

o   By including specific details, you can add layers of depth and nuance to your images, making them richer and more visually appealing.

3. **Reducing Misinterpretation**:

o   Ambiguous or vague prompts can lead to unintended results. Detailed descriptions minimize the chances of misinterpretation by providing clear and specific instructions.

Components of Detailed Descriptions

A detailed prompt typically includes several key components:

1. **Subject**:

o   Identify the main focus of your image clearly.

2. **Action**:

o   Describe what the subject is doing.

3. **Setting and Context**:

o   Provide information about the environment or background.

4. **Attributes and Descriptors**:

o   Include specific characteristics, such as colors, textures, emotions, and styles.

Examples of Detailed Descriptions

Example 1: Person

- **Vague**: "A woman"

- **Detailed**: "A young woman with long, curly brown hair, wearing a red dress with white polka dots, standing on a bustling city street at sunset, holding a bouquet of sunflowers"

Breakdown:

- **Subject**: "A young woman"

- **Action**: "standing"

- **Setting and Context**: "on a bustling city street at sunset"

- **Attributes and Descriptors**: "long, curly brown hair," "wearing a red dress with white polka dots," "holding a bouquet of sunflowers"

Example 2: Scene

- **Vague**: "A forest"

- **Detailed**: "A dense forest with towering pine trees, their needles creating a soft carpet on the forest floor, dappled sunlight filtering through the canopy, and a clear, babbling brook winding through the underbrush"

Breakdown:

- **Subject**: "A dense forest"

- **Setting and Context**: "towering pine trees," "soft carpet on the forest floor," "dappled sunlight filtering through the canopy," "a clear, babbling brook winding through the underbrush"

Example 3: Object

- **Vague**: "A book"

- **Detailed**: "An ancient, leather-bound book with gilded edges and an ornate, embossed cover, resting on an antique wooden desk under a soft, warm light from a nearby lamp"

Breakdown:

- **Subject**: "An ancient, leather-bound book"

- **Setting and Context**: "resting on an antique wooden desk"

- **Attributes and Descriptors**: "with gilded edges," "ornate, embossed cover," "under a soft, warm light from a nearby lamp"

Practical Tips for Writing Detailed Descriptions

1. **Use Sensory Details**:

o Engage the senses by describing how things look, sound, feel, smell, or taste. This creates a more immersive and vivid image.

Example:

- "A cozy living room with a crackling fireplace, the scent of pine in the air, soft woolen blankets draped over a plush sofa, and the sound of raindrops tapping on the windowpane"

2. **Be Specific with Numbers and Measurements**:

o Including specific numbers and measurements adds precision to your descriptions.

Example:

- "A grand dining table set for eight, with a centerpiece of fresh roses in a crystal vase, and plates arranged in a symmetrical pattern"

3. **Incorporate Emotions and Moods**:

o Describe the emotions or mood you want the image to convey.

Example:

- "A serene lakeside scene at dawn, with mist rising from the water, and the soft glow of the rising sun casting a tranquil, golden light"

4. **Describe Relationships and Interactions**:

o Highlight how different elements in the scene interact with each other.

Example:

- "A mother and child playing in a park, the child laughing as they run through a field of wildflowers, with the mother watching lovingly"

Crafting Descriptive Prompts

Crafting descriptive prompts is essential for guiding AI tools like Midjourney to generate high-quality and accurate images. Descriptive prompts provide the AI with detailed and vivid information about the desired image, reducing ambiguity and ensuring that the output aligns with your vision. This section will explore techniques for crafting effective descriptive prompts and provide examples to illustrate these techniques.

Techniques for Crafting Descriptive Prompts

1. **Use Vivid Adjectives and Adverbs**

o Incorporate descriptive language to paint a clear and detailed picture for the AI. Adjectives and adverbs help to specify the qualities and characteristics of the subject, action, and setting.

Example:

o Instead of "a tree," describe "a towering oak tree with lush, green leaves swaying gently in the breeze."

2. **Specify Actions and Interactions**

o Clearly describe what the subjects are doing and how they are interacting with their environment. This adds dynamism and context to the image.

Example:

o Instead of "a dog," describe "a playful golden retriever chasing a red ball across a grassy field."

3. **Include Context and Setting**

o Provide detailed information about the environment or background where the scene is taking place. This adds depth and richness to the image.

Example:

o Instead of "a person," describe "a young woman sitting on a park bench, reading a book under the shade of a cherry blossom tree in full bloom."

4. **Incorporate Sensory Details**

o   Engage the senses by describing how things look, sound, feel, smell, or taste. This creates a more immersive and vivid image.

Example:

o   Instead of "a market," describe "a bustling marketplace filled with the aroma of fresh spices, the vibrant colors of fruits and vegetables, and the lively chatter of vendors and customers."

5.   **Use Similes and Metaphors**

o   Employ similes and metaphors to create strong visual associations and enhance the descriptive quality of the prompt.

Example:

o   Instead of "a sunset," describe "a fiery sunset painting the sky in shades of orange and pink, like a canvas set ablaze."

6.   **Provide Specific Numbers and Measurements**

o   Including specific numbers and measurements adds precision to your descriptions and helps the AI generate more accurate images.

Example:

o   Instead of "a crowd," describe "a crowd of hundreds of people, tightly packed together, cheering and waving flags."

7.   **Incorporate Emotions and Moods**

o   Describe the emotions or mood you want the image to convey. This helps the AI capture the intended atmosphere and tone.

Example:

o   Instead of "a street," describe "a quiet, cobblestone street bathed in the soft glow of streetlights, evoking a sense of calm and nostalgia."

Examples of Descriptive Prompts

Example 1: Nature Scene

- **Simple Prompt**: "A mountain"

- **Descriptive Prompt**: "A majestic snow-capped mountain rising above a serene valley, with pine trees lining the slopes and a crystal-clear river flowing at its base"

Breakdown:

- **Subject**: "A majestic snow-capped mountain"

- **Setting and Context**: "rising above a serene valley," "pine trees lining the slopes," "a crystal-clear river flowing at its base"

- **Attributes and Descriptors**: "majestic," "snow-capped," "serene," "crystal-clear"

Example 2: Urban Scene

- **Simple Prompt**: "A city street"

- **Descriptive Prompt**: "A bustling city street at dusk, with neon signs illuminating the storefronts, cars honking in traffic, and pedestrians hurrying along the sidewalks, their faces lit by the warm glow of streetlights"

Breakdown:

- **Subject**: "A bustling city street"

- **Setting and Context**: "at dusk," "neon signs illuminating the storefronts," "cars honking in traffic," "pedestrians hurrying along the sidewalks"

- **Attributes and Descriptors**: "bustling," "dusk," "neon signs," "warm glow of streetlights"

Example 3: Character Portrait

- **Simple Prompt**: "A knight"

- **Descriptive Prompt**: "A valiant knight in shining armor, mounted on a powerful white steed, holding a gleaming sword aloft, with a castle looming in the background under a stormy sky"

Breakdown:

- **Subject**: "A valiant knight"

- **Action**: "mounted on a powerful white steed," "holding a gleaming sword aloft"

- **Setting and Context**: "with a castle looming in the background," "under a stormy sky"

- **Attributes and Descriptors**: "valiant," "shining armor," "powerful white steed," "gleaming sword," "stormy sky"

Crafting descriptive prompts is essential for generating high-quality images with AI tools like Midjourney. By using vivid adjectives and adverbs, specifying actions and interactions, including context and setting, incorporating sensory details, using similes and metaphors, providing specific numbers and measurements, and describing emotions and moods, you can create detailed and vivid prompts that guide the AI effectively. Mastering these techniques will enhance your ability to communicate your creative vision and achieve stunning visual results.

<u>Using Adjectives and Adverbs Effectively</u>

Adjectives and adverbs are powerful tools in crafting descriptive prompts. They add depth, color, and nuance to your descriptions, helping the AI to generate more vivid and accurate images. Effective use of these modifiers can transform a simple prompt into a rich, detailed narrative, guiding the AI to produce the desired visual output.

The Role of Adjectives and Adverbs

1. **Adjectives**:

o Adjectives describe or modify nouns, providing more information about the subject's qualities, appearance, size, shape, and other characteristics.

2. **Adverbs**:

o Adverbs modify verbs, adjectives, or other adverbs, giving additional details about how, when, where, or to what extent something is happening.

Techniques for Using Adjectives and Adverbs Effectively

1. **Be Specific**:

o Use specific adjectives and adverbs to create a clear and precise image. Avoid vague or general terms.

Example:

o Instead of "a big dog," use "a large, muscular German Shepherd."

2. **Avoid Redundancy**:

o Choose adjectives and adverbs that add new information rather than repeating what is already implied.

Example:

o Instead of "a tall, towering skyscraper," use "a towering skyscraper."

3. **Use Sensory Descriptions**:

o   Engage the senses by describing how things look, sound, feel, smell, or taste.

Example:

o   Instead of "a forest," use "a dense forest with the fresh scent of pine and the soft rustle of leaves in the breeze."

4. **Combine Adjectives and Adverbs**:

o   Use multiple adjectives and adverbs together to provide a fuller picture, but ensure they complement each other.

Example:

o   "A swiftly moving river with clear, sparkling water flowing over smooth, rounded stones."

5. **Balance Detail and Clarity**:

o   While details are important, ensure that your descriptions remain clear and easy to understand.

Example:

o   Instead of "a very old and extremely weathered wooden bench," use "an ancient, weathered wooden bench."

Examples of Effective Use of Adjectives and Adverbs

Example 1: Describing a Scene

- **Simple Prompt**: "A garden"

- **Descriptive Prompt**: "A lush, vibrant garden filled with blooming flowers of every color, the sweet fragrance of roses and jasmine wafting through the air, and bees buzzing busily among the blossoms."

Breakdown:

- **Adjectives**: "lush," "vibrant," "blooming," "every color," "sweet," "busy"

- **Adverbs**: "wafting," "buzzing"

Example 2: Describing a Person

- **Simple Prompt**: "A woman"

- **Descriptive Prompt**: "A graceful, elderly woman with silvery hair tied in a neat bun, wearing a flowing, lavender dress, and walking slowly through a sunlit park."

Breakdown:

- **Adjectives**: "graceful," "elderly," "silvery," "neat," "flowing," "lavender," "sunlit"

- **Adverbs**: "slowly"

Example 3: Describing an Object

- **Simple Prompt**: "A book"

- **Descriptive Prompt**: "An ancient, leather-bound book with intricately embossed covers, its yellowed pages filled with delicate, handwritten script."

Breakdown:

- **Adjectives**: "ancient," "leather-bound," "intricately embossed," "yellowed," "delicate," "handwritten"

- **Adverbs**: None needed here, as the adjectives provide sufficient detail.

Practical Tips for Effective Use

1. **Vary Your Vocabulary:**

- o Use a diverse range of adjectives and adverbs to keep your descriptions fresh and engaging. Avoid repetition and overuse of common words.

Example:

- o Instead of repeatedly using "beautiful," try "stunning," "gorgeous," "breathtaking," "exquisite."

2. **Context Matters**:

- o Choose adjectives and adverbs that fit the context of your scene. Ensure they enhance the overall mood and atmosphere you wish to create.

Example:

- o For a dark, eerie forest, use "gloomy," "shadowy," "creeping," "whispering."

3. **Consistency**:

- o Ensure that your adjectives and adverbs are consistent with the overall theme and tone of your prompt.

Example:

- o For a serene beach scene, use "calm," "gentle," "soft," "tranquil."

4. **Avoid Overloading**:

- o While detailed descriptions are valuable, too many adjectives and adverbs can clutter your prompt and make it difficult for the AI to focus on the main elements.

Example:

- o Instead of "a beautiful, large, old, white, wooden house," use "a charming, old white house with a spacious porch."

Adjectives and adverbs are essential tools for crafting detailed and vivid prompts that guide AI tools like Midjourney effectively. By using specific, sensory, and context-appropriate descriptions, you can create clear and engaging prompts that lead to high-quality, accurate images. Balancing detail with clarity and avoiding redundancy ensures that your prompts are both descriptive and easy for the AI to interpret, enhancing the overall quality of the generated images.

Examples of Descriptive vs. Vague Prompts

The quality of AI-generated images largely depends on the clarity and specificity of the prompts provided. Vague prompts can lead to unpredictable and generic results, whereas descriptive prompts guide the AI to produce detailed and accurate images.

Examples of Descriptive vs. Vague Prompts

Example 1: Nature Scene

- **Vague Prompt**: "A mountain"

- **Descriptive Prompt**: "A majestic snow-capped mountain rising above a serene valley, with pine trees lining the slopes and a crystal-clear river flowing at its base"

Analysis:

- The vague prompt "a mountain" could result in any generic mountain image.

- The descriptive prompt provides specific details about the mountain's appearance, the surrounding environment, and additional elements like the pine trees and river, creating a vivid and precise image.

Example 2: Urban Scene

- **Vague Prompt**: "A city street"

- **Descriptive Prompt**: "A bustling city street at dusk, with neon signs illuminating the storefronts, cars honking in traffic, and pedestrians hurrying along the sidewalks, their faces lit by the warm glow of streetlights"

Analysis:

- The vague prompt "a city street" lacks detail and context, resulting in a generic urban image.

- The descriptive prompt adds depth by specifying the time of day, lighting, sounds, and activities, creating a more engaging and realistic scene.

Example 3: Character Portrait

- **Vague Prompt**: "A knight"

- **Descriptive Prompt**: "A valiant knight in shining armor, mounted on a powerful white steed, holding a gleaming sword aloft, with a castle looming in the background under a stormy sky"

Analysis:

- The vague prompt "a knight" provides minimal information, leading to a wide range of possible interpretations.

- The descriptive prompt specifies the knight's appearance, actions, and the setting, resulting in a detailed and dynamic image.

Example 4: Animal

- **Vague Prompt**: "A cat"

- **Descriptive Prompt**: "A sleek black cat with piercing green eyes, sitting gracefully on a sunlit windowsill, its tail curled around its body"

Analysis:

- The vague prompt "a cat" can lead to any generic cat image.

- The descriptive prompt details the cat's appearance, pose, and setting, creating a more specific and visually interesting image.

Example 5: Object

- **Vague Prompt**: "A book"

- **Descriptive Prompt**: "An ancient, leather-bound book with intricately embossed covers, resting on an antique wooden desk under a soft, warm light from a nearby lamp"

Analysis:

- The vague prompt "a book" is too general and could refer to any type of book.

- The descriptive prompt includes details about the book's age, material, design, and the setting, providing a clear and rich visual.

Example 6: Scene

- **Vague Prompt**: "A beach"

- **Descriptive Prompt**: "A tranquil beach at sunset, with golden sand, gentle waves lapping at the shore, and palm trees silhouetted against a fiery orange sky"

Analysis:

- The vague prompt "a beach" lacks specific details and context.

- The descriptive prompt adds elements like the time of day, colors, and natural features, creating a vivid and appealing image.

Practical Tips for Creating Descriptive Prompts

1. **Include Specific Details**:

o Add as many relevant details as possible about the subject, setting, and other elements. This helps the AI understand your vision more clearly.

Example:

o Instead of "a flower," describe "a bright red rose with dewdrops on its petals, blooming in a well-tended garden."

2. **Use Descriptive Language**:

o Utilize adjectives and adverbs to provide more information about the qualities and characteristics of the scene or object.

Example:

o Instead of "a house," describe "a quaint cottage with a thatched roof, surrounded by blooming wildflowers and a white picket fence."

3. **Set the Scene**:

o Provide context and background to enrich the image and give it depth.

Example:

o Instead of "a boat," describe "a small wooden boat drifting peacefully on a crystal-clear lake, with mist rising from the water in the early morning light."

4. **Engage the Senses**:

o   Describe sensory details to create a more immersive and vivid image.

Example:

o   Instead of "a forest," describe "a dense forest with the earthy smell of damp soil and pine needles, the sound of birds chirping, and dappled sunlight filtering through the canopy."

Crafting detailed and descriptive prompts is crucial for guiding AI tools like Midjourney to produce high-quality and accurate images. By transforming vague prompts into rich, detailed descriptions, you can provide the AI with the information it needs to generate images that closely match your creative vision. This approach not only enhances the accuracy of the output but also creates more engaging and visually appealing images.

Conclusion

Detailed descriptions are essential for creating accurate, nuanced, and visually rich AI-generated images. By including specific details about the subject, action, setting, and attributes, you provide the AI with clear and precise instructions, reducing ambiguity and enhancing the quality of the output. Mastering the art of detailed descriptions will significantly improve your ability to communicate your creative vision and achieve stunning visual results with Midjourney.

Chapter 4: Using Parameters

Midjourney allows users to fine-tune the generated images by using various parameters. These parameters provide control over aspects such as image composition, style, and quality, enabling users to achieve more precise and desired outcomes. Understanding how to use these parameters effectively can significantly enhance the quality and specificity of the AI-generated images.

Key Parameters and Their Uses

1. **Aspect Ratio (--ar)**

The aspect ratio parameter controls the width-to-height ratio of the generated image. This is useful for creating images that fit specific dimensions, such as widescreen wallpapers, square social media posts, or portrait-oriented illustrations.

Usage:

- --ar 16:9 for a widescreen format

- --ar 1:1 for a square format

- --ar 9:16 for a portrait format

Example:

- Prompt: "A serene mountain landscape at sunrise"

- With Aspect Ratio: "A serene mountain landscape at sunrise --ar 16:9"

2. **Chaos (--chaos)**

The chaos parameter introduces randomness and variation into the generated images. Higher values result in more diverse and experimental outputs, while lower values produce more consistent and controlled results.

Usage:

- --chaos 0 for minimal variation

- --chaos 100 for maximum variation

Example:

- Prompt: "A futuristic cityscape at night"

- With Chaos: "A futuristic cityscape at night --chaos 50"

3. **Quality (--q)**

The quality parameter adjusts the rendering quality and detail of the generated images. Higher quality values result in more detailed and refined images but may take longer to generate.

Usage:

- --q 1 for standard quality

- --q 2 for high quality

- --q 0.5 for lower quality

Example:

- Prompt: "A detailed close-up of a lion's face"

- With Quality: "A detailed close-up of a lion's face --q 2"

4. **Stylize (--stylize)**

The stylize parameter influences the artistic style applied to the generated image. Higher values result in more stylized and artistic outputs, while lower values produce more realistic images.

Usage:

- --stylize 0 for realistic images

- --stylize 1000 for highly stylized images

Example:

- Prompt: "A portrait of a medieval knight"

- With Stylize: "A portrait of a medieval knight --stylize 500"

5. **Seed (--seed)**

   The seed parameter allows users to generate similar images by specifying a seed number. Using the same seed number with the same prompt will produce similar outputs, which is useful for consistency across multiple images.

Usage:

- --seed 12345

Example:

- Prompt: "A magical forest with glowing mushrooms"

- With Seed: "A magical forest with glowing mushrooms --seed 67890"

Combining Parameters

   Users can combine multiple parameters in a single prompt to achieve even more precise control over the generated images. This allows for detailed customization and fine-tuning.

Example:

- Prompt: "A fantasy castle on a hilltop at sunset"

- Combined Parameters: "A fantasy castle on a hilltop at sunset --ar 16:9 --chaos 25 --q 2 --stylize 700 --seed 54321"

Practical Tips for Using Parameters

1. **Experiment with Different Values**:

   o Try various values for each parameter to see how they affect the output. Experimentation helps in understanding the impact of each parameter and finding the perfect combination for your needs.

2. **Start Simple**:

   o Begin with a basic prompt and gradually add parameters. This approach allows you to see the incremental changes and better understand how each parameter influences the final image.

3. **Iterate and Refine**:

   o Use iterative refinement to tweak parameters based on the results. Adjust values incrementally and regenerate images to achieve the desired outcome.

4. **Balance Quality and Speed**:

   o Higher quality images take longer to generate. Balance the quality parameter with your time constraints to optimize both the image detail and generation speed.

5. **Leverage Community Insights**:

   o Learn from examples and tips shared by the Midjourney community. Seeing how others use parameters can provide valuable insights and inspire new approaches.

Overview of Key Parameters

Aspect Ratio (--ar)

Aspect ratio is a critical parameter in Midjourney that determines the width-to-height ratio of the generated image. This parameter is essential for ensuring that the generated images fit specific formats and use cases, whether for social media, print, or digital art. Understanding how to use the --ar parameter effectively allows users to control the composition and layout of their images, making them suitable for various applications.

Understanding Aspect Ratio

The aspect ratio is expressed as two numbers separated by a colon, such as 16:9, 1:1, or 4:3. These numbers represent the proportional relationship between the width and height of the image. Adjusting the aspect ratio changes the shape of the image, which can significantly impact its composition and visual appeal.

Common Aspect Ratios and Their Uses

1. **16:9 (Widescreen)**

The 16:9 aspect ratio is widely used for widescreen displays, including televisions, computer monitors, and online videos. It provides a broad and cinematic view, making it ideal for landscapes, cityscapes, and panoramic scenes.

Example:

- Prompt: "A serene mountain landscape at sunrise"

- With Aspect Ratio: "A serene mountain landscape at sunrise --ar 16:9"

Use Case:

- Ideal for YouTube thumbnails, desktop wallpapers, and cinematic scenes.

2. **1:1 (Square)**

The 1:1 aspect ratio produces a square image, commonly used on social media platforms like Instagram. It offers a balanced and centered composition, suitable for portraits, detailed close-ups, and minimalist designs.

Example:

- Prompt: "A close-up of a blooming red rose"

- With Aspect Ratio: "A close-up of a blooming red rose --ar 1:1"

Use Case:

- Perfect for Instagram posts, profile pictures, and product images.

3. **4:3 (Standard)**

The 4:3 aspect ratio is traditionally used in photography and older television screens. It offers a more compact and balanced view, making it suitable for portraits, documentary photography, and educational content.

Example:

- Prompt: "A family portrait in a garden"

- With Aspect Ratio: "A family portrait in a garden --ar 4:3"

Use Case:

- Useful for printed photographs, educational materials, and portrait-oriented content.

4. **9:16 (Portrait)**

The 9:16 aspect ratio is commonly used for vertical formats, such as smartphone screens and social media stories. It provides a tall and narrow view, ideal for full-body portraits, tall buildings, and vertical panoramas.

Example:

- Prompt: "A tall skyscraper against a clear blue sky"

- With Aspect Ratio: "A tall skyscraper against a clear blue sky -- ar 9:16"

Use Case:

- Best for Instagram Stories, TikTok videos, and mobile wallpapers.

Practical Examples and Applications

Example 1: Landscape Scene

- **Prompt**: "A beautiful beach at sunset"

- **Without Aspect Ratio**: "A beautiful beach at sunset"

- **With Aspect Ratio (16:9)**: "A beautiful beach at sunset --ar 16:9"

o **Explanation**: The widescreen format captures the expansive view of the beach and the setting sun, enhancing the scenic beauty.

Example 2: Portrait

- **Prompt**: "A smiling child holding a balloon"

- **Without Aspect Ratio**: "A smiling child holding a balloon"

- **With Aspect Ratio (1:1)**: "A smiling child holding a balloon --ar 1:1"

o **Explanation**: The square format centers the child and balloon, creating a balanced and engaging portrait.

Example 3: Product Image

- **Prompt**: "A stylish wristwatch on a marble surface"

- **Without Aspect Ratio**: "A stylish wristwatch on a marble surface"

- **With Aspect Ratio (4:3)**: "A stylish wristwatch on a marble surface --ar 4:3"

o **Explanation**: The standard format highlights the wristwatch details and provides a professional presentation suitable for catalogs.

Example 4: Vertical Panorama

- **Prompt**: "A majestic waterfall cascading down a cliff"

- **Without Aspect Ratio**: "A majestic waterfall cascading down a cliff"

- **With Aspect Ratio (9:16)**: "A majestic waterfall cascading down a cliff --ar 9:16"

o **Explanation**: The vertical format captures the height and grandeur of the waterfall, making it ideal for mobile viewing.

Tips for Using Aspect Ratio

1. **Match the Medium**:

o Choose an aspect ratio that fits the intended medium or platform. For example, use 16:9 for YouTube thumbnails and 1:1 for Instagram posts.

2. **Enhance Composition**:

o Use aspect ratios to enhance the composition of your image. A wider ratio can emphasize landscapes, while a taller ratio can highlight vertical subjects.

3. **Consider the Audience**:

o Think about how your audience will view the image. Mobile users may prefer vertical formats, while desktop users might favor widescreen views.

4. **Experiment with Different Ratios**:

o Don't hesitate to experiment with different aspect ratios to see how they affect the overall look and feel of the image. This can lead to discovering new and interesting compositions.

The aspect ratio (--ar) parameter is a powerful tool in Midjourney that allows users to control the width-to-height ratio of their generated images. By understanding and utilizing common aspect ratios like 16:9, 1:1, 4:3, and 9:16, users can tailor their images to fit specific formats and enhance their visual impact. Experimenting with different aspect ratios and matching them to the intended medium and audience can significantly improve the quality and relevance of AI-generated images.

Chaos (--chaos)

The --chaos parameter in Midjourney is a powerful tool that controls the level of randomness and variation in the generated images. By adjusting the chaos level, users can influence how experimental or consistent the outputs are. This parameter is particularly useful for exploring a range of creative possibilities and achieving the desired balance between unpredictability and precision in the generated images.

Understanding Chaos

The --chaos parameter accepts values ranging from 0 to 100. Lower values produce more predictable and consistent results, while higher values introduce greater randomness and variation. This allows users to experiment with different levels of chaos to find the perfect balance for their creative needs.

Key Concepts

1. **Low Chaos (0-20):**

   o Produces consistent and controlled images with minimal variation.

   o Suitable for scenarios where precision and accuracy are important.

2. **Medium Chaos (21-50):**

   o Introduces moderate variation, offering a balance between consistency and creativity.

   o Useful for adding a touch of unpredictability without losing control over the final output.

3. **High Chaos (51-100):**

   o Generates highly varied and experimental images with significant randomness.

   o Ideal for exploring unconventional and creative designs, where unexpected results can lead to unique and interesting outcomes.

Examples of Using Chaos

Example 1: Landscape Scene

- **Prompt**: "A serene mountain landscape at sunrise"

1. **Low Chaos**:

- o Prompt with Low Chaos: "A serene mountain landscape at sunrise --chaos 10"

- o **Result**: A consistent and detailed depiction of a mountain landscape with minimal variation between generated images.

2. **Medium Chaos**:

- o Prompt with Medium Chaos: "A serene mountain landscape at sunrise --chaos 30"

- o **Result**: Variations in the landscape features, such as different mountain shapes, lighting effects, and color tones, while maintaining the overall theme.

3. **High Chaos**:

- o Prompt with High Chaos: "A serene mountain landscape at sunrise --chaos 70"

- o **Result**: Highly varied images with significant differences in mountain formations, dramatic lighting changes, and diverse color palettes.

Example 2: Character Portrait

- **Prompt**: "A futuristic warrior in a neon-lit city"

1. **Low Chaos**:

- o Prompt with Low Chaos: "A futuristic warrior in a neon-lit city --chaos 10"

- o **Result**: Consistent portrayals of the warrior with similar poses, attire, and background elements.

2. **Medium Chaos**:

o Prompt with Medium Chaos: "A futuristic warrior in a neon-lit city --chaos 40"

o **Result**: Variations in the warrior's appearance, such as different armor designs, lighting effects, and cityscape details.

3. **High Chaos**:

o Prompt with High Chaos: "A futuristic warrior in a neon-lit city --chaos 80"

o **Result**: Highly diverse interpretations, including different warrior poses, experimental armor designs, and dynamic cityscapes with a wide range of neon colors.

Example 3: Abstract Art

• **Prompt**: "An abstract painting with swirling colors"

1. **Low Chaos**:

o Prompt with Low Chaos: "An abstract painting with swirling colors --chaos 5"

o **Result**: Controlled and harmonious compositions with consistent color patterns and swirl formations.

2. **Medium Chaos**:

o Prompt with Medium Chaos: "An abstract painting with swirling colors --chaos 35"

o **Result**: A balanced mix of predictable and unexpected elements, with moderate variation in color swirls and patterns.

3. **High Chaos**:

o   Prompt with High Chaos: "An abstract painting with swirling colors --chaos 90"

o   **Result**: Wildly varied and experimental artworks with unpredictable color combinations and dynamic swirl patterns.

Practical Tips for Using Chaos

1. **Start with Medium Chaos**:

o   Begin with a medium chaos level (around 30-50) to explore a balance between consistency and creativity. Adjust based on the results to either increase or decrease variation.

2. **Refine Through Iteration**:

o   Use iterative refinement to fine-tune the chaos level. Generate multiple images with different chaos settings to find the ideal balance for your specific project.

3. **Match the Project Requirements**:

o   Adjust the chaos level according to the requirements of your project. Use low chaos for professional and precise images, medium chaos for balanced creativity, and high chaos for experimental and artistic endeavors.

4. **Combine with Other Parameters**:

o   Enhance the creative possibilities by combining the chaos parameter with other parameters like aspect ratio, quality, and stylize. This allows for more comprehensive control over the final output.

The --chaos parameter in Midjourney is a versatile tool that allows users to control the level of randomness and variation in their generated images. By understanding and effectively using this parameter, users can explore a wide range of creative possibilities, from highly consistent and controlled images to experimental and unpredictable artworks. Experimenting with different levels of chaos and combining it with other parameters can significantly enhance the quality and uniqueness of AI-generated images.

Stylize (--stylize)

The --stylize parameter in Midjourney is an essential tool for influencing the artistic style of generated images. By adjusting the stylize level, users can control the degree to which artistic and creative elements are incorporated into the images. This parameter ranges from producing highly realistic images to generating highly stylized and artistic outputs. Understanding how to use the --stylize parameter effectively allows users to tailor the visual aesthetic of their images to match specific creative visions.

Understanding Stylize

The --stylize parameter accepts values ranging from 0 to 1000. Lower values result in more realistic and less stylized images, while higher values introduce more artistic elements and creativity, making the images more stylized and less true-to-life.

Key Concepts

1. **Low Stylize (0-100):**

o   Produces realistic images with minimal artistic influence.

o   Suitable for scenarios where accuracy and realism are important.

2. **Medium Stylize (101-500):**

o   Introduces a balance between realism and artistic style.

o   Useful for adding creative flair while maintaining a degree of realism.

3. **High Stylize (501-1000):**

- o Generates highly stylized and artistic images with significant creative elements.

- o Ideal for artistic projects where creativity and visual impact are prioritized over realism.

Examples of Using Stylize

Example 1: Nature Scene

- **Prompt**: "A serene mountain landscape at sunrise"

1. **Low Stylize**:

- o Prompt with Low Stylize: "A serene mountain landscape at sunrise --stylize 50"

- o **Result**: A realistic depiction of a mountain landscape with accurate colors and details.

2. **Medium Stylize**:

- o Prompt with Medium Stylize: "A serene mountain landscape at sunrise --stylize 300"

- o **Result**: A balanced image with enhanced colors and slight artistic touches, such as more vibrant lighting and smoother transitions.

3. **High Stylize**:

- o Prompt with High Stylize: "A serene mountain landscape at sunrise --stylize 800"

- o **Result**: A highly artistic representation with exaggerated colors, dramatic lighting, and impressionistic details.

Example 2: Character Portrait

- **Prompt**: "A futuristic warrior in a neon-lit city"

1. **Low Stylize**:

o Prompt with Low Stylize: "A futuristic warrior in a neon-lit city --stylize 100"

o **Result**: A realistic portrait with detailed armor, lifelike facial features, and accurate lighting effects.

2. **Medium Stylize**:

o Prompt with Medium Stylize: "A futuristic warrior in a neon-lit city --stylize 400"

o **Result**: A portrait with enhanced neon lighting, smoother textures, and more stylized armor design.

3. **High Stylize**:

o Prompt with High Stylize: "A futuristic warrior in a neon-lit city --stylize 900"

o **Result**: A highly creative and artistic portrait with exaggerated neon effects, bold colors, and abstract elements.

Example 3: Abstract Art

• **Prompt**: "An abstract painting with swirling colors"

1. **Low Stylize**:

o Prompt with Low Stylize: "An abstract painting with swirling colors --stylize 50"

o **Result**: A controlled and somewhat realistic representation of swirling colors.

2. **Medium Stylize**:

o Prompt with Medium Stylize: "An abstract painting with swirling colors --stylize 400" o **Result**: A vibrant and dynamic painting with pronounced swirling patterns and a mix of realistic and artistic elements.

3. **High Stylize**:

o Prompt with High Stylize: "An abstract painting with swirling colors --stylize 900"

o **Result**: An intensely stylized and creative artwork with dramatic swirls, bold color contrasts, and highly abstract forms.

Practical Tips for Using Stylize

1. **Start with Medium Stylize**:

o Begin with a medium stylize level (around 300-500) to explore a balance between realism and creativity. Adjust based on the results to either increase or decrease the stylization.

2. **Match the Artistic Intent**:

o Choose a stylize level that fits the intended artistic style of your project. Use low stylize for realistic images, medium stylize for balanced creativity, and high stylize for highly artistic and abstract images.

3. **Combine with Other Parameters**:

o Enhance the visual impact by combining the stylize parameter with other parameters like aspect ratio, chaos, and quality. This allows for more comprehensive control over the final output.

4. **Experiment with Different Styles**:

o Don't hesitate to experiment with various stylize levels to see how they affect the overall look and feel of the image. This can lead to discovering new and interesting artistic styles.

The --stylize parameter in Midjourney is a versatile tool that allows users to control the level of artistic influence in their generated images. By understanding and effectively using this parameter, users can create a wide range of visual styles, from highly realistic to intensely artistic and abstract. Experimenting with different levels of stylization and combining it with other parameters can significantly enhance the aesthetic quality and uniqueness of AI-generated images.

Practical Applications of Parameters

The use of parameters in Midjourney allows for precise control over various aspects of image generation, such as composition, style, and randomness. Understanding practical applications of these parameters can help users achieve their creative goals more effectively.

Aspect Ratio (--ar)

Practical Application: Adjusting the aspect ratio is crucial for creating images that fit specific formats and purposes, such as social media posts, desktop wallpapers, and print layouts.

Example:

- **Prompt**: "A tranquil beach scene"

- **Standard Aspect Ratio (1:1)**: "A tranquil beach scene --ar 1:1"

  o **Use Case**: Ideal for Instagram posts, offering a balanced and centered composition.

- **Widescreen Aspect Ratio (16:9)**: "A tranquil beach scene --ar 16:9"

- o **Use Case**: Suitable for desktop wallpapers or YouTube thumbnails, providing a broad and cinematic view.

Chaos (--chaos)

Practical Application: The chaos parameter is used to introduce varying levels of randomness and experimentation in the generated images. This is useful for exploring creative variations and achieving a desired level of unpredictability.

Example:

- **Prompt**: "A futuristic cityscape at night"

- **Low Chaos (10)**: "A futuristic cityscape at night --chaos 10"

- o **Result**: Consistent and detailed depictions with minimal variation.

- o **Use Case**: Ideal for professional or precise imagery where consistency is key.

- **High Chaos (70)**: "A futuristic cityscape at night --chaos 70"

- o **Result**: Highly varied and experimental images with significant differences in elements and style.

- o **Use Case**: Useful for artistic projects where creativity and uniqueness are prioritized.

Quality (--q)

Practical Application: The quality parameter controls the level of detail and rendering time for the generated images. Higher quality settings result in more detailed and refined images but may take longer to generate.

Example:

- **Prompt**: "A detailed portrait of an elderly man"

- **Standard Quality (--q 1)**: "A detailed portrait of an elderly man --q 1"

o **Result**: Good quality images with a balance of detail and generation time.

o **Use Case**: Suitable for most uses, providing a reasonable level of detail.

- **High Quality (--q 2)**: "A detailed portrait of an elderly man --q 2"

o **Result**: Highly detailed and refined images with longer rendering times.

o **Use Case**: Ideal for high-resolution prints or close-up views where detail is paramount.

Stylize (--stylize)

Practical Application: The stylize parameter influences the artistic style of the images, ranging from realistic to highly artistic and abstract. This is useful for matching the visual aesthetic to specific creative visions.

Example:

- **Prompt**: "An enchanted forest"

- **Low Stylize (--stylize 50)**: "An enchanted forest --stylize 50"

o **Result**: Realistic depiction with minimal artistic influence.

o **Use Case**: Suitable for realistic scenes and professional uses.

- **High Stylize (--stylize 800)**: "An enchanted forest --stylize 800"

o **Result**: Highly artistic and abstract images with exaggerated features and colors.

- o **Use Case**: Ideal for creative projects where a unique and artistic style is desired.

Seed (--seed)

Practical Application: The seed parameter allows users to generate similar images by specifying a seed number. This is useful for creating consistent themes across multiple images.

Example:

- **Prompt**: "A bustling marketplace"

- **With Seed (--seed 12345)**: "A bustling marketplace --seed 12345"

- o **Result**: Consistent images with similar composition and elements.

- o **Use Case**: Ideal for series of images or themed projects where consistency is important.

Combining Parameters

Practical Application: Combining multiple parameters allows for comprehensive control over the generated images, enabling fine-tuning to meet specific creative needs.

Example:

- **Prompt**: "A fantasy castle on a hill at sunset"

- **Combined Parameters**: "A fantasy castle on a hill at sunset --ar 16:9 --chaos 30 --q 2 --stylize 500 --seed 67890"

- o **Result**: A high-quality, stylized image with a wide aspect ratio and moderate variation.

- o **Use Case**: Suitable for a fantasy-themed project, providing a detailed and creative depiction that fits widescreen formats.

Understanding and applying parameters in Midjourney can greatly enhance the quality and specificity of AI-generated images. By adjusting parameters like aspect ratio, chaos, quality, stylize, and seed, users can tailor the output to match their creative visions and practical requirements. Experimenting with different combinations of these parameters allows for a wide range of possibilities, enabling the creation of unique and visually compelling images.

Step-by-Step Guide to Using Parameters

Using parameters effectively in Midjourney can significantly enhance the quality and specificity of the generated images. This step-by-step guide will walk you through the process of applying key parameters such as aspect ratio, chaos, quality, stylize, and seed. Each step includes examples to illustrate how these parameters can be combined to achieve desired results.

Step 1: Basic Prompt Creation

Start with a basic prompt that describes the image you want to generate. Ensure your prompt is clear and specific to provide a solid foundation for applying parameters.

Example:

- Basic Prompt: "A serene mountain landscape at sunrise"

Step 2: Adjusting Aspect Ratio (--ar)

The aspect ratio parameter controls the width-to-height ratio of the image. Choose an aspect ratio that fits your desired format.

Usage:

- --ar <width>:<height>

Example:

- Prompt with Aspect Ratio: "A serene mountain landscape at sunrise --ar 16:9"

  o **Explanation**: This sets the image to a widescreen format, ideal for desktop wallpapers or YouTube thumbnails.

Step 3: Applying Chaos (--chaos)

The chaos parameter introduces randomness and variation. Adjust this to control the level of unpredictability in the generated images.

Usage:

- --chaos <value>

Example:

- Prompt with Chaos: "A serene mountain landscape at sunrise --ar 16:9 --chaos 30"

  o **Explanation**: This adds moderate variation to the image, allowing for creative differences while maintaining a consistent theme.

Step 4: Setting Quality (--q)

The quality parameter controls the detail and rendering time. Higher values produce more detailed images but may take longer to generate.

Usage:

- --q <value>

Example:

- Prompt with Quality: "A serene mountain landscape at sunrise --ar 16:9 --chaos 30 --q 2"

- o **Explanation**: This increases the image quality, making it more detailed and refined, suitable for high-resolution prints.

Step 5: Influencing Style with Stylize (--stylize)

The stylize parameter determines the level of artistic influence. Higher values make the image more creative and stylized.

Usage:

- --stylize <value>

Example:

- Prompt with Stylize: "A serene mountain landscape at sunrise --ar 16:9 --chaos 30 --q 2 --stylize 500"

- o **Explanation**: This adds a significant artistic touch, enhancing colors and forms to create a more stylized and visually appealing image.

Step 6: Ensuring Consistency with Seed (--seed)

The seed parameter ensures consistency across multiple images by using the same random seed value. This is useful for generating similar images.

Usage:

- --seed <value>

Example:

- Prompt with Seed: "A serene mountain landscape at sunrise --ar 16:9 --chaos 30 --q 2 --stylize 500 --seed 12345"

  - o **Explanation**: This ensures that the generated images are consistent, making it ideal for projects requiring a uniform visual style.

Step 7: Combining Parameters

Combining multiple parameters allows for fine-tuned control over the generated image. Experiment with different combinations to achieve the desired effect.

Example:

- Comprehensive Prompt: "A serene mountain landscape at sunrise --ar 16:9 --chaos 30 --q 2 --stylize 500 --seed 12345"

- **Explanation**: This prompt combines aspect ratio, chaos, quality, stylize, and seed parameters to create a high-quality, stylized image with consistent variations.

Practical Example: Creating a Fantasy Castle Scene

1. **Basic Prompt**:

- "A fantasy castle on a hill at sunset"

2. **Adding Aspect Ratio**:

- "A fantasy castle on a hill at sunset --ar 16:9"

- **Use Case**: Widescreen format for a cinematic view.

3. **Introducing Chaos**:

- "A fantasy castle on a hill at sunset --ar 16:9 --chaos 40"

- **Use Case**: Adds creative variations to the castle and landscape.

4. **Enhancing Quality**:

- "A fantasy castle on a hill at sunset --ar 16:9 --chaos 40 --q 2"

- **Use Case**: Increases detail for a high-resolution output.

5. **Applying Stylize**:

- o "A fantasy castle on a hill at sunset --ar 16:9 --chaos 40 --q 2 --stylize 600"

- o **Use Case**: Adds an artistic touch, making the scene more magical.

6. **Setting Seed**:

- o "A fantasy castle on a hill at sunset --ar 16:9 --chaos 40 --q 2 --stylize 600 --seed 78910"

- o **Use Case**: Ensures consistency across multiple generated images.

Using parameters effectively in Midjourney allows for precise control over the generated images. By following this step-by-step guide, you can enhance your prompts with aspect ratio, chaos, quality, stylize, and seed parameters, achieving high-quality, creative, and consistent results. Experimenting with different combinations of these parameters will help you unlock the full potential of Midjourney and bring your creative visions to life.

Conclusion

Using parameters effectively in Midjourney allows for greater control and customization of AI-generated images. By understanding and experimenting with parameters like aspect ratio, chaos, quality, stylize, and seed, users can fine-tune their prompts to achieve more precise, detailed, and creative outputs. Mastering these parameters enhances the ability to communicate your creative vision and produce stunning visual content.

Chapter 5: Enhancing Creativity with Synonyms

One effective way to enhance creativity in prompt writing for Midjourney is by using synonyms. Synonyms add variety to your language, prevent repetition, and can inspire the AI to generate more diverse and imaginative images. By varying your word choices, you can unlock new creative possibilities and achieve richer, more nuanced results.

Why Use Synonyms?

1. **Avoid Repetition**:

o   Using the same words repeatedly can make your prompts monotonous. Synonyms introduce variety, keeping your descriptions fresh and engaging.

2. **Expand Creativity**:

o   Different words can evoke different images and associations. By experimenting with synonyms, you can explore a broader range of visual possibilities.

3. **Refine Descriptions**:

o   Synonyms allow you to fine-tune your descriptions, making them more precise and effective in conveying your creative vision.

4. **Stimulate the AI**:

o   Varied language can stimulate the AI in different ways, leading to more diverse and unexpected outputs.

Examples of Using Synonyms in Prompts

Example 1: Describing a Scene

- **Basic Prompt**: "A beautiful garden"
- **Enhanced with Synonyms**:
  o "A picturesque garden"
  o "A charming garden"
  o "A delightful garden"

Analysis:

- By using synonyms like "picturesque," "charming," and "delightful," you can evoke different nuances and visual elements in the AI-generated images.

Example 2: Describing a Person

- **Basic Prompt**: "A happy child"
- **Enhanced with Synonyms**:
  o "A joyful child"
  o "A cheerful child"
  o "A gleeful child"

Analysis:

- Synonyms like "joyful," "cheerful," and "gleeful" provide subtle variations in the emotional tone, which can influence the AI to generate different expressions and body language.

Example 3: Describing an Object

- **Basic Prompt**: "A shiny car"
- **Enhanced with Synonyms**:
  o "A gleaming car"

- o "A polished car"

- o "A lustrous car"

Analysis:

- Words like "gleaming," "polished," and "lustrous" each bring out different qualities of shine and reflectiveness, leading to varied interpretations by the AI.

Practical Tips for Using Synonyms

1. **Use a Thesaurus**:

- o A thesaurus is a valuable tool for finding synonyms. Use it to explore different word choices that can enhance your prompts.

2. **Consider Context**:

- o Ensure that the synonyms you choose fit the context of your prompt. Some words may carry different connotations or nuances that might not be appropriate for every scenario.

3. **Experiment with Variations**:

- o Don't be afraid to experiment with different synonyms in your prompts. Generate multiple versions of an image using different word choices to see how the AI responds.

4. **Combine Synonyms**:

- o Combine multiple synonyms in a single prompt to add depth and richness to your descriptions.

Example:

- "A serene and tranquil lake surrounded by lush and verdant greenery"

Analysis:

- Using both "serene" and "tranquil" as well as "lush" and "verdant" enhances the description, creating a more vivid and detailed image.

Examples of Enhanced Prompts with Synonyms

Example 1: Nature Scene

- **Basic Prompt**: "A quiet forest"

- **Enhanced Prompt**: "A peaceful and silent forest with towering, ancient trees and a carpet of emerald-green moss"

Analysis:

- Synonyms like "peaceful" and "silent" add layers of calmness, while "towering" and "ancient" provide a sense of grandeur and history.

Example 2: Urban Scene

- **Basic Prompt**: "A busy street"

- **Enhanced Prompt**: "A bustling and lively street filled with vibrant shops and energetic pedestrians"

Analysis:

- Words like "bustling," "lively," "vibrant," and "energetic" convey a dynamic and active atmosphere, enhancing the visual richness of the scene.

Example 3: Character Portrait

- **Basic Prompt**: "A wise old man"

- **Enhanced Prompt**: "A sagacious and venerable old man with piercing eyes and a thoughtful expression"

Analysis:

- Synonyms such as "sagacious" and "venerable" elevate the description, adding depth to the character's wisdom and presence.

The Power of Synonyms in Prompt Writing

Synonyms are words or phrases that have similar meanings. They are a powerful tool in prompt writing, enabling writers to add variety, nuance, and depth to their descriptions. Utilizing synonyms effectively can enhance the creativity of your prompts, making the resulting AI-generated images more vivid, diverse, and engaging.

The Power of Synonyms

1. **Adding Variety**:

o   Repeated use of the same words can make descriptions monotonous. Synonyms introduce variety, making your prompts more interesting and engaging for the AI to interpret.

2. **Nuance and Precision**:

o   Different synonyms carry different connotations and levels of intensity. Choosing the right synonym can convey the exact nuance or emotion you want, leading to more precise and expressive images.

3. **Stimulating Creativity**:

o   Using varied language can stimulate the AI in different ways, resulting in a wider range of interpretations and more creative outputs.

4. **Expanding Descriptive Possibilities**:

o   Synonyms allow you to explore different aspects of a scene or object, adding layers of detail and depth to your descriptions.

Examples of Using Synonyms in Prompt Writing

Example 1: Describing a Scene

- **Basic Prompt**: "A beautiful garden"

- **Enhanced with Synonyms**:

  o "A picturesque garden"

  o "A charming garden"

  o "A delightful garden"

Analysis:

- Synonyms like "picturesque," "charming," and "delightful" each evoke slightly different visual and emotional responses, leading the AI to generate varied interpretations of a garden.

Example 2: Describing a Person

- **Basic Prompt**: "A happy child"

- **Enhanced with Synonyms**:

  o "A joyful child"

  o "A cheerful child"

  o "A gleeful child"

Analysis:

- Words like "joyful," "cheerful," and "gleeful" convey different shades of happiness, which can influence the AI to depict different expressions, body language, and scenarios.

Example 3: Describing an Object

- **Basic Prompt**: "A shiny car"

- **Enhanced with Synonyms**:

  o "A gleaming car"

  o "A polished car"

  o "A lustrous car"

Analysis:

- Synonyms such as "gleaming," "polished," and "lustrous" highlight different aspects of shininess, such as reflectiveness or surface quality, resulting in diverse visual outputs.

Practical Tips for Using Synonyms

1. **Thesaurus Use**:

   o A thesaurus is an excellent tool for finding synonyms. It helps you discover alternative words that can add variety and precision to your prompts.

2. **Contextual Fit**:

   o Ensure that the synonyms you choose fit the context of your prompt. Some words might have different connotations or intensities that may not be appropriate for every scenario.

3. **Experimentation**:

   o Experiment with different synonyms in your prompts. Generate multiple versions of an image using varied language to see how the AI responds and which words produce the best results.

4. **Combining Synonyms**:

   o Use multiple synonyms within a single prompt to create rich, multi-layered descriptions.

Example:

- "A serene and tranquil lake surrounded by lush and verdant greenery"

Analysis:

- Combining "serene" and "tranquil" as well as "lush" and "verdant" enhances the description, providing a more detailed and vivid image.

Enhanced Prompts with Synonyms

Example 1: Nature Scene

- **Basic Prompt**: "A quiet forest"

- **Enhanced Prompt**: "A peaceful and silent forest with towering, ancient trees and a carpet of emerald-green moss"

Analysis:

- Synonyms like "peaceful" and "silent" add layers of calmness, while "towering" and "ancient" provide a sense of grandeur and history.

Example 2: Urban Scene

- **Basic Prompt**: "A busy street"

- **Enhanced Prompt**: "A bustling and lively street filled with vibrant shops and energetic pedestrians"

Analysis:

- Words like "bustling," "lively," "vibrant," and "energetic" convey a dynamic and active atmosphere, enhancing the visual richness of the scene.

Example 3: Character Portrait

- **Basic Prompt**: "A wise old man"

- **Enhanced Prompt**: "A sagacious and venerable old man with piercing eyes and a thoughtful expression"

Analysis:

- Synonyms such as "sagacious" and "venerable" elevate the description, adding depth to the character's wisdom and presence.

The power of synonyms in prompt writing lies in their ability to add variety, nuance, and depth to descriptions. By incorporating a range of synonyms, you can enhance the creativity and expressiveness of your prompts, leading to richer and more diverse AI-generated images. Experimenting with different synonyms and combining them effectively will enrich your descriptions and stimulate the AI to produce a broader range of visual interpretations.

Tools and Techniques for Finding Synonyms

Using synonyms effectively in prompt writing can greatly enhance the creativity and richness of AI-generated images. Finding the right synonyms involves a combination of tools and techniques that can help you discover alternative words that add variety, nuance, and depth to your descriptions.

Tools for Finding Synonyms

1. **Thesaurus**

A thesaurus is an essential tool for discovering synonyms. It lists words along with their synonyms and antonyms, providing a quick way to find alternative expressions.

Examples:

- **Thesaurus.com**: An online thesaurus offering a wide range of synonyms.

  o **Basic Word**: "Beautiful"

  o **Synonyms**: "Attractive," "Gorgeous," "Stunning," "Charming"

2. **Online Synonym Generators**

These tools generate a list of synonyms for any given word, often providing additional context and usage examples.

Examples:

- **Power Thesaurus**: A crowdsourced online thesaurus with a vast collection of synonyms.

  o **Basic Word**: "Happy"

  o **Synonyms**: "Joyful," "Cheerful," "Content," "Pleased"

3. **Writing Assistance Tools**

Tools like Grammarly and ProWritingAid offer synonym suggestions while you write, helping you enhance your vocabulary on the go.

Examples:

- **Grammarly**: Offers synonym suggestions as you type, helping to improve the richness of your writing.

  o **Basic Word**: "Quick"

  o **Synonyms**: "Fast," "Rapid," "Swift," "Speedy"

4. **Language Translation Tools**

Translation tools like Google Translate can provide synonyms in different languages, which can then be translated back to discover new and unique word choices.

Examples:

- **Google Translate**: Translate a word to another language and back to find alternative synonyms.

o **Basic Word**: "Strong"

o **Translated to Spanish and Back**: "Robust," "Sturdy," "Vigorous"

Techniques for Finding Synonyms

1. **Contextual Understanding**

Ensure that the synonyms fit the context of your prompt. Words with similar meanings can have different connotations and usage scenarios.

Example:

- **Basic Prompt**: "A serene lake"

o **Contextual Synonyms**: "A tranquil lake," "A peaceful lake," "A calm lake"

2. **Exploring Different Shades of Meaning**

Synonyms can vary in intensity and nuance. Choose synonyms that precisely convey the desired intensity and emotion.

Example:

- **Basic Word**: "Happy"

o **Shades of Meaning**:

- Mild: "Content"

- Moderate: "Cheerful"

- Strong: "Ecstatic"

3. Combining Synonyms

Combine multiple synonyms in a single prompt to add depth and richness.

Example:

- **Basic Prompt**: "A beautiful garden"

o **Enhanced Prompt**: "A picturesque and charming garden"

4. Using Analogies and Metaphors

Think of analogies and metaphors that convey similar meanings, then find synonyms for those analogies.

Example:

- **Basic Word**: "Bright"

o **Analogies**: "Shining like the sun"

o **Synonyms**: "Radiant," "Luminous," "Brilliant"

Practical Examples of Enhanced Prompts

Example 1: Nature Scene

- **Basic Prompt**: "A beautiful sunset"

- **Enhanced with Synonyms**:

o "A stunning and breathtaking sunset with hues of orange and pink spreading across the sky"

Example 2: Character Description

- **Basic Prompt**: "A wise old man"

- **Enhanced with Synonyms**:

- o "A sagacious and venerable old man with deep, thoughtful eyes and a gentle demeanor"

Example 3: Urban Scene

- **Basic Prompt**: "A busy marketplace"

- **Enhanced with Synonyms**:

- o "A bustling and vibrant marketplace filled with energetic vendors and colorful stalls"

Using synonyms is a powerful technique for enhancing creativity in prompt writing. By utilizing tools like thesauruses, online synonym generators, writing assistance tools, and translation services, you can discover a wide range of synonyms that add variety and depth to your descriptions. Techniques such as understanding context, exploring shades of meaning, combining synonyms, and using analogies further refine your prompts, resulting in richer and more nuanced AI-generated images. Experimenting with these tools and techniques will significantly enhance your ability to craft creative and engaging prompts.

Examples and Case Studies

Using synonyms effectively can transform simple prompts into rich, evocative descriptions that inspire more creative and diverse AI-generated images.

Examples of Synonyms in Prompt Writing

Example 1: Nature Scene

- **Basic Prompt**: "A beautiful garden"

- **Enhanced with Synonyms**:

- o "A picturesque garden"

- o "A charming garden"

- o "A delightful garden"

Impact:

- Using synonyms like "picturesque," "charming," and "delightful" creates different nuances and visual interpretations of a garden. "Picturesque" might evoke a garden that's visually appealing in a traditional or artistic sense, while "charming" suggests a cozy, inviting atmosphere, and "delightful" conveys a sense of joy and pleasure.

Example 2: Character Description

- **Basic Prompt**: "A wise old man"

- **Enhanced with Synonyms**:

- o "A sagacious old man"

- o "A venerable old man"

- o "A sage-like old man"

Impact:

- Synonyms such as "sagacious," "venerable," and "sage-like" each highlight different aspects of wisdom. "Sagacious" emphasizes intelligence and discernment, "venerable" suggests respect and honor due to age and character, and "sage-like" conveys a more mystical or philosophical quality.

Example 3: Urban Scene

- **Basic Prompt**: "A busy street"

- **Enhanced with Synonyms**:

- o "A bustling street"

- o "A lively street"

- o "A vibrant street"

Impact:

- Words like "bustling," "lively," and "vibrant" infuse the scene with energy and activity, but each carries a slightly different connotation. "Bustling" indicates a lot of movement and noise, "lively" suggests a cheerful and dynamic atmosphere, and "vibrant" implies vividness and excitement.

Case Studies

Case Study 1: Transforming a Landscape Scene

Initial Prompt:

- "A peaceful lake at sunset"

Enhanced Prompt:

- "A tranquil and serene lake at sunset with golden reflections dancing on the water and the distant mountains bathed in a warm, orange glow"

Analysis:

- By using synonyms like "tranquil" and "serene" along with additional descriptive elements, the prompt becomes richer and more evocative. The use of "golden reflections" and "warm, orange glow" adds visual and sensory details that guide the AI to create a more compelling and nuanced image.

Case Study 2: Character Enhancement

Initial Prompt:

- "A fierce warrior"

Enhanced Prompt:

- "A formidable and intrepid warrior clad in gleaming armor, with a determined gaze and a battle-hardened stance"

Analysis:

- Synonyms like "formidable" and "intrepid" enhance the depiction of the warrior, emphasizing strength and bravery. Adding specific details about the warrior's appearance and demeanor further enriches the prompt, leading to a more detailed and dynamic image.

Case Study 3: Urban Vibrancy

Initial Prompt:

- "A colorful market"

Enhanced Prompt:

- "A vibrant and bustling market brimming with colorful stalls, fragrant spices, and the lively chatter of vendors and shoppers"

Analysis:

- Using "vibrant" and "bustling" to describe the market adds energy and vividness. Specific details about the stalls, spices, and sounds create a more immersive scene, encouraging the AI to generate a rich and detailed image of a lively market.

Practical Examples and Comparisons

Example 1: Animal Description

- **Basic Prompt**: "A cute puppy"

- **Enhanced with Synonyms**:

o   "An adorable and playful puppy with fluffy fur and sparkling eyes"

Comparison:

- "Adorable" and "playful" add depth to the description of the puppy, while "fluffy fur" and "sparkling eyes" provide visual details that make the image more engaging.

Example 2: Artistic Scene

- **Basic Prompt**: "A colorful painting"

- **Enhanced with Synonyms**:

o   "A vibrant and dynamic painting with bold brushstrokes and a kaleidoscope of hues"

Comparison:

- "Vibrant" and "dynamic" convey energy and movement, while "bold brushstrokes" and "kaleidoscope of hues" add artistic details that enrich the visual representation.

Using synonyms in prompt writing is a powerful technique for enhancing creativity and enriching descriptions. Through the examples and case studies presented, it's evident that varied word choices can significantly impact the resulting AI-generated images, making them more diverse, nuanced, and engaging. By experimenting with synonyms and incorporating them thoughtfully into your prompts, you can unlock new creative possibilities and achieve more detailed and imaginative results.

Conclusion

Enhancing creativity with synonyms is a powerful technique in prompt writing for Midjourney. By incorporating varied and precise language, you can unlock new creative possibilities and achieve more detailed and imaginative AI-generated images. Experimenting with synonyms and combining them effectively in your prompts will enrich your descriptions and stimulate the AI to produce a wider range of visual interpretations.

Chapter 6: Positive Language in Prompts

The language used in prompts plays a crucial role in shaping the output of AI-generated images. Positive language, in particular, can enhance the clarity, tone, and overall quality of the prompts, leading to more desirable and visually appealing results.

The Importance of Positive Language

1. **Clarity and Precision**:

o   Positive language helps in conveying clear and precise instructions. It avoids ambiguity and confusion, making it easier for the AI to interpret the prompt accurately.

2. **Enhanced Creativity**:

o   Using positive and descriptive words stimulates creativity, encouraging the AI to generate more vivid and imaginative images.

3. **Avoiding Misinterpretations**:

o   Negative language or instructions can sometimes lead to unintended results. Positive language ensures that the prompt focuses on what should be included, rather than what should be avoided.

4. **Emotional Tone**:

o   Positive language sets a constructive and engaging tone, which can be reflected in the mood and atmosphere of the generated image.

Techniques for Using Positive Language

1. **Focus on Inclusion**:

o   Describe what should be included in the image rather than what should be excluded.

Example:

• Instead of "a street without cars," use "a pedestrian-friendly street with cafes and shops."

2. **Use Descriptive Adjectives**:

o   Employ positive and descriptive adjectives to enhance the imagery.

Example:

• Instead of "a small room," use "a cozy, sunlit room with a comfortable armchair."

3. **Highlight Positive Actions and Interactions**:

o   Focus on positive actions and interactions to create a more engaging scene.

Example:

• Instead of "people not arguing," use "people enjoying a lively conversation."

4. **Emphasize Positive Attributes**:

o   Highlight the positive attributes of the subject, setting, or objects in the prompt.

Example:

• Instead of "a dark alley," use "a charming alley illuminated by string lights."

Examples of Positive Language in Prompts

Example 1: Describing a Scene

- **Negative Prompt**: "A park without litter"

- **Positive Prompt**: "A clean and well-maintained park with blooming flowers and green lawns"

Analysis:

- The positive prompt emphasizes the desirable aspects of the park, creating a more vivid and appealing image.

Example 2: Character Description

- **Negative Prompt**: "A person not frowning"

- **Positive Prompt**: "A person with a bright smile and cheerful demeanor"

Analysis:

- Focusing on the positive attributes of the person's expression enhances the emotional tone and clarity of the prompt.

Example 3: Urban Scene

- **Negative Prompt**: "A street without traffic"

- **Positive Prompt**: "A bustling pedestrian street with lively cafes and street performers"

Analysis:

- The positive prompt highlights the vibrancy and activity of the street, creating a more engaging and dynamic image.

Practical Tips for Using Positive Language

1. **Reframe Negative Statements**:

   o Reframe negative statements into positive descriptions by focusing on what you want to see in the image.

Example:

- Instead of "a building without graffiti," use "a beautifully painted building with vibrant murals."

2. **Be Specific and Descriptive**:

o Use specific and descriptive language to provide clear and detailed instructions.

Example:

- Instead of "a good view," use "a panoramic view of the sunset over the mountains."

3. **Highlight Desirable Features**:

o Emphasize the desirable features of the subject, setting, or objects in the prompt.

Example:

- Instead of "an area without noise," use "a tranquil garden with the gentle sound of birds chirping."

Enhanced Prompts with Positive Language

Example 1: Nature Scene

- **Negative Prompt**: "A beach without crowds"

- **Positive Prompt**: "A serene and secluded beach with crystal-clear water and soft white sand"

Analysis:

- The positive prompt emphasizes the peaceful and attractive qualities of the beach, making the image more appealing.

Example 2: Character Portrait

- **Negative Prompt**: "A person not looking sad"

- **Positive Prompt**: "A joyful person with sparkling eyes and a radiant smile"

Analysis:

- The positive prompt focuses on the positive emotions and expressions, enhancing the clarity and emotional tone of the image.

Example 3: Artistic Scene

- **Negative Prompt**: "An artwork without dull colors"

- **Positive Prompt**: "A vibrant and colorful artwork with bold brushstrokes and dynamic composition"

Analysis:

- The positive prompt highlights the desired artistic elements, creating a more vivid and engaging image.

Why Avoid Negative Language

The language used in prompts significantly influences the outcome of AI-generated images. Negative language can lead to ambiguity, misinterpretation, and unintended results. In contrast, positive language provides clear, precise instructions that guide the AI effectively.

The Pitfalls of Negative Language

1. **Ambiguity and Misinterpretation**:

   o Negative language often leaves room for ambiguity. Phrases like "without," "not," or "avoid" can confuse the AI, leading to results that do not align with the intended vision.

2. **Focus on the Undesired**:

o   Negative language emphasizes what should not be included, rather than what should be. This can detract from the main focus and dilute the effectiveness of the prompt.

3. **Complex Processing**:

o   AI models process positive and direct instructions more effectively. Negative instructions require additional cognitive processing, increasing the likelihood of errors.

4. **Reduced Creativity**:

o   Negative prompts can limit the creative potential of the AI by restricting its ability to explore and generate diverse interpretations.

Examples of Negative vs. Positive Language

Example 1: Describing a Scene

- **Negative Prompt**: "A park without litter"

- **Positive Prompt**: "A clean and well-maintained park with blooming flowers and green lawns"

Analysis:

- The negative prompt emphasizes the absence of litter, which can be ambiguous. The positive prompt focuses on desirable attributes, providing clear and vivid details.

Example 2: Character Description

- **Negative Prompt**: "A person not frowning"

- **Positive Prompt**: "A person with a bright smile and cheerful demeanor"

Analysis:

- The negative prompt highlights what should not be present, which can confuse the AI. The positive prompt clearly describes the desired expression and mood.

Example 3: Urban Scene

- **Negative Prompt**: "A street without traffic"

- **Positive Prompt**: "A bustling pedestrian street with lively cafes and street performers"

Analysis:

- The negative prompt focuses on the absence of traffic, which might lead to a bland image. The positive prompt describes a vibrant and engaging scene.

Practical Tips for Avoiding Negative Language

1. **Reframe Negative Statements**:

o Convert negative statements into positive descriptions by focusing on what should be included.

Example:

- Instead of "a building without graffiti," use "a beautifully painted building with vibrant murals."

2. **Emphasize Positive Attributes**:

o Highlight the positive aspects of the subject, setting, or objects in the prompt.

Example:

- Instead of "a dark alley," use "a charming alley illuminated by string lights."

3. **Be Specific and Descriptive**:

o   Use specific and descriptive language to provide clear and detailed instructions.

Example:

*   Instead of "a good view," use "a panoramic view of the sunset over the mountains."

Enhanced Prompts with Positive Language

Example 1: Nature Scene

*   **Negative Prompt**: "A beach without crowds"

*   **Positive Prompt**: "A serene and secluded beach with crystal-clear water and soft white sand"

Analysis:

*   The positive prompt emphasizes the peaceful and attractive qualities of the beach, making the image more appealing.

Example 2: Character Portrait

*   **Negative Prompt**: "A person not looking sad"

*   **Positive Prompt**: "A joyful person with sparkling eyes and a radiant smile"

Analysis:

*   The positive prompt focuses on the positive emotions and expressions, enhancing the clarity and emotional tone of the image.

Example 3: Artistic Scene

*   **Negative Prompt**: "An artwork without dull colors"

- **Positive Prompt**: "A vibrant and colorful artwork with bold brushstrokes and dynamic composition"

Analysis:

- The positive prompt highlights the desired artistic elements, creating a more vivid and engaging image.

Avoiding negative language in prompts is essential for achieving clear, precise, and creative AI-generated images. Negative language can lead to ambiguity, misinterpretation, and reduced creativity. By reframing negative statements, emphasizing positive attributes, and using specific and descriptive language, you can create more effective prompts that guide the AI to produce visually appealing and accurate results.

Techniques for Rephrasing Prompts Positively

Using positive language in prompts is crucial for achieving clear, precise, and desirable outcomes in AI-generated images. Positive language focuses on what should be included rather than what should be avoided, guiding the AI more effectively.

Techniques for Rephrasing Prompts Positively

1. **Focus on Inclusion**

One effective technique for rephrasing prompts positively is to focus on what should be included in the scene, rather than what should be excluded. This provides clear guidance to the AI and reduces ambiguity.

Example:

- **Negative Prompt**: "A park without litter"

- **Positive Prompt**: "A clean and well-maintained park with blooming flowers and green lawns"

Analysis:

- The positive prompt emphasizes desirable attributes, creating a more vivid and appealing image.

2. **Highlight Positive Attributes**

Instead of mentioning what should not be present, highlight the positive attributes of the subject, setting, or objects in the prompt. This creates a constructive and engaging tone.

Example:

- **Negative Prompt**: "A person not frowning"

- **Positive Prompt**: "A person with a bright smile and cheerful demeanor"

Analysis:

- Focusing on positive attributes enhances the clarity and emotional tone of the image.

3. **Use Descriptive Adjectives**

Employ positive and descriptive adjectives to enhance the imagery and provide detailed instructions.

Example:

- **Negative Prompt**: "A small room"

- **Positive Prompt**: "A cozy, sunlit room with a comfortable armchair"

Analysis:

- Descriptive adjectives like "cozy" and "sunlit" create a more inviting and detailed image.

4. **Reframe Negative Statements**

Convert negative statements into positive descriptions by focusing on what you want to see in the image.

Example:

- **Negative Prompt**: "A street without traffic"

- **Positive Prompt**: "A bustling pedestrian street with lively cafes and street performers"

Analysis:

- The positive prompt describes a vibrant and engaging scene, enhancing the visual appeal.

5. **Be Specific and Descriptive**

Use specific and descriptive language to provide clear and detailed instructions. This reduces ambiguity and guides the AI more effectively.

Example:

- **Negative Prompt**: "A dark alley"

- **Positive Prompt**: "A charming alley illuminated by string lights"

Analysis:

- Specific and descriptive language creates a more vivid and appealing image.

Practical Examples of Rephrasing Prompts Positively

Example 1: Nature Scene

- **Negative Prompt**: "A beach without crowds"

- **Positive Prompt**: "A serene and secluded beach with crystal-clear water and soft white sand"

Analysis:

- The positive prompt emphasizes the peaceful and attractive qualities of the beach, making the image more appealing.

Example 2: Character Portrait

- **Negative Prompt**: "A person not looking sad"

- **Positive Prompt**: "A joyful person with sparkling eyes and a radiant smile"

Analysis:

- Focusing on positive emotions and expressions enhances the clarity and emotional tone of the image.

Example 3: Artistic Scene

- **Negative Prompt**: "An artwork without dull colors"

- **Positive Prompt**: "A vibrant and colorful artwork with bold brushstrokes and dynamic composition"

Analysis:

- The positive prompt highlights the desired artistic elements, creating a more vivid and engaging image.

Using positive language in prompts is essential for guiding AI to produce clear, precise, and visually appealing images. Techniques such as focusing on inclusion, highlighting positive attributes, using descriptive adjectives, reframing negative statements, and being specific and descriptive can significantly enhance the quality of prompts. By applying these techniques, you can create more effective prompts that lead to desirable and creative outcomes in AI-generated images.

Examples and Best Practices

Using positive language in prompts is a powerful technique for generating clear, engaging, and visually appealing AI-generated images. Positive prompts guide the AI by emphasizing what should be included, rather than what should be avoided.

Examples of Positive Language in Prompts

Example 1: Describing a Scene

- **Negative Prompt**: "A park without litter"

- **Positive Prompt**: "A clean and well-maintained park with blooming flowers and green lawns"

Analysis:

- The positive prompt provides clear and specific details about the desired state of the park, emphasizing cleanliness and beauty.

Example 2: Character Description

- **Negative Prompt**: "A person not frowning"

- **Positive Prompt**: "A person with a bright smile and cheerful demeanor"

Analysis:

- By focusing on the positive attributes of the person's expression, the prompt creates a more vivid and engaging image.

Example 3: Urban Scene

- **Negative Prompt**: "A street without traffic"

- **Positive Prompt**: "A bustling pedestrian street with lively cafes and street performers"

Analysis:

- The positive prompt highlights the vibrancy and activity of the street, making the scene more dynamic and interesting.

Best Practices for Using Positive Language

1. **Focus on What to Include**

Emphasize what should be present in the scene rather than what should be absent. This approach provides clear instructions to the AI and avoids ambiguity.

Example:

- **Negative Prompt**: "A building without graffiti"

- **Positive Prompt**: "A beautifully painted building with vibrant murals"

2. **Use Descriptive Adjectives**

Incorporate positive and descriptive adjectives to enhance the imagery and provide more detail.

Example:

- **Negative Prompt**: "A small room"

- **Positive Prompt**: "A cozy, sunlit room with a comfortable armchair"

3. **Highlight Positive Actions and Interactions**

Describe positive actions and interactions to create engaging and lively scenes.

Example:

- **Negative Prompt**: "People not arguing"

- **Positive Prompt**: "People enjoying a lively conversation"

4. **Reframe Negative Statements**

Convert negative statements into positive descriptions by focusing on what you want to see.

Example:

- **Negative Prompt**: "A street without noise"

- **Positive Prompt**: "A peaceful street with the gentle hum of distant chatter and birds singing"

5. **Be Specific and Detailed**

Provide specific and detailed descriptions to guide the AI more effectively.

Example:

- **Negative Prompt**: "A good view"

- **Positive Prompt**: "A panoramic view of the sunset over the mountains, with hues of orange and pink spreading across the sky"

Enhanced Prompts with Positive Language

Example 1: Nature Scene

- **Negative Prompt**: "A beach without crowds"

- **Positive Prompt**: "A serene and secluded beach with crystal-clear water and soft white sand"

Analysis:

- The positive prompt emphasizes the peaceful and attractive qualities of the beach, making the image more appealing.

Example 2: Character Portrait

- **Negative Prompt**: "A person not looking sad"

- **Positive Prompt**: "A joyful person with sparkling eyes and a radiant smile"

Analysis:

- Focusing on positive emotions and expressions enhances the clarity and emotional tone of the image.

Example 3: Artistic Scene

- **Negative Prompt**: "An artwork without dull colors"

- **Positive Prompt**: "A vibrant and colorful artwork with bold brushstrokes and dynamic composition"

Analysis:

- The positive prompt highlights the desired artistic elements, creating a more vivid and engaging image.

Using positive language in prompts is essential for generating clear, engaging, and visually appealing AI-generated images. By focusing on what to include, using descriptive adjectives, highlighting positive actions and interactions, reframing negative statements, and being specific and detailed, you can create more effective prompts that lead to desirable and creative outcomes. Incorporating these best practices into your prompt writing will enhance both the clarity and creativity of the resulting images.

Conclusion

Using positive language in prompts is a powerful technique that enhances the clarity, creativity, and emotional tone of AI-generated images. By focusing on what should be included and emphasizing positive attributes, you can create more vivid, engaging, and visually appealing results. Reframing negative statements, being specific and descriptive, and highlighting desirable features are key strategies for incorporating positive language into your prompt writing.

Chapter 7: Embracing Ambiguity and Creativity

While clarity and specificity are important in prompt writing, embracing ambiguity can unlock a higher level of creativity. Allowing some level of vagueness can inspire the AI to interpret prompts in unique and unexpected ways, leading to more diverse and innovative outputs.

The Role of Ambiguity in Creativity

1. **Fostering Innovation**:

   o Ambiguity encourages the AI to explore various interpretations, resulting in creative and novel images that might not arise from overly specific prompts.

2. **Stimulating Imagination**:

   o Ambiguous prompts leave room for interpretation, prompting the AI to fill in the gaps with imaginative and inventive elements.

3. **Encouraging Exploration**:

   o By not prescribing every detail, ambiguous prompts allow the AI to experiment with different styles, compositions, and themes, enhancing the diversity of the generated images.

Techniques for Embracing Ambiguity

1. **Open-Ended Descriptions**:

o Use descriptions that provide a general idea without specifying every detail. This approach encourages the AI to explore different possibilities.

   Example:

- **Specific Prompt**: "A red barn on a green field under a blue sky"

- **Ambiguous Prompt**: "A countryside scene"

Analysis:

- The ambiguous prompt allows the AI to interpret what constitutes a countryside scene, resulting in a variety of possible images.

2. **Suggestive Language**:

o Use language that suggests rather than dictates. Words like "perhaps," "might," or "could" introduce a sense of possibility and openness.

Example:

- **Specific Prompt**: "A woman in a red dress holding a blue umbrella"

- **Ambiguous Prompt**: "A woman, perhaps holding something colorful, standing in the rain"

Analysis:

- The suggestive language allows the AI to experiment with different interpretations of what the woman might be holding and how she is depicted.

3. **Abstract Concepts**:

o Incorporate abstract concepts that can be interpreted in multiple ways. This encourages the AI to explore a range of visual representations.

Example:

- **Specific Prompt**: "A cat sitting on a windowsill"

- **Ambiguous Prompt**: "A moment of tranquility"

Analysis:

- The abstract concept "a moment of tranquility" can be visualized in countless ways, leading to diverse and creative outputs.

4. **Minimalist Prompts**:

o Provide minimal details to encourage maximum creative freedom for the AI. This can lead to unexpected and innovative results.

Example:

- **Specific Prompt**: "A bustling city street with people, cars, and shops"

- **Ambiguous Prompt**: "Urban life"

Analysis:

- The minimalist prompt "urban life" allows the AI to interpret and visualize the concept in various ways, from street scenes to skyline views.

Practical Examples of Ambiguous Prompts

Example 1: Nature Scene

- **Specific Prompt**: "A forest with tall pine trees and a clear stream"

- **Ambiguous Prompt**: "A hidden sanctuary in nature"

Analysis:

- The ambiguous prompt encourages the AI to imagine different kinds of natural sanctuaries, leading to varied and potentially unexpected results.

Example 2: Character Description

- **Specific Prompt**: "A knight in shining armor on a white horse"

- **Ambiguous Prompt**: "A figure of courage"

Analysis:

- The abstract prompt "a figure of courage" can be interpreted in numerous ways, from traditional knights to modern-day heroes.

Example 3: Artistic Scene

- **Specific Prompt**: "A modern art painting with geometric shapes and bold colors"

- **Ambiguous Prompt**: "An expression of chaos and order"

Analysis:

- The ambiguous prompt encourages the AI to explore different artistic styles and compositions that represent the interplay of chaos and order.

Benefits of Embracing Ambiguity

1. **Enhanced Diversity**:

o Ambiguous prompts lead to a wider range of outputs, enhancing the diversity and richness of the generated images.

2. **Unexpected Innovations**:

o By allowing the AI to interpret the prompt creatively, you may discover unexpected and innovative visual solutions.

3. **Greater Artistic Freedom**:

o Ambiguity gives the AI more freedom to experiment, leading to more dynamic and original images.

Benefits of Leaving Room for Interpretation

Embracing ambiguity in prompt writing can lead to more creative, diverse, and innovative AI-generated images. By intentionally leaving room for interpretation, you allow the AI to explore various possibilities, resulting in unexpected and original outputs.

Benefits of Leaving Room for Interpretation

1. **Fostering Innovation**

When prompts are less rigid and more open-ended, the AI is encouraged to explore different interpretations and possibilities. This freedom fosters innovation, leading to the creation of unique and original images.

Example:

- **Specific Prompt**: "A cat sitting on a red sofa in a living room"

- **Ambiguous Prompt**: "A cozy moment at home with a pet"

Analysis:

- The ambiguous prompt "A cozy moment at home with a pet" allows the AI to explore various cozy home scenes, potentially featuring different pets and settings, leading to innovative interpretations.

2. **Encouraging Diverse Outputs**

Ambiguity in prompts can result in a wider range of outputs. By not specifying every detail, you invite the AI to experiment with different elements, styles, and compositions, enhancing the diversity of the generated images.

Example:

- **Specific Prompt**: "A mountain with snow-covered peaks and a clear blue sky"

- **Ambiguous Prompt**: "A majestic landscape"

Analysis:

- The ambiguous prompt "A majestic landscape" can be interpreted in numerous ways, including mountains, forests, lakes, or other natural scenes, leading to a variety of outputs.

3. **Stimulating Creative Problem-Solving**

Leaving room for interpretation challenges the AI to fill in the gaps creatively. This can result in more imaginative solutions and artistic representations, as the AI navigates the ambiguity to generate a coherent image.

Example:

- **Specific Prompt**: "A busy marketplace with vendors selling fruits"

- **Ambiguous Prompt**: "A bustling hub of activity"

Analysis:

- The ambiguous prompt "A bustling hub of activity" allows the AI to explore different busy scenes, such as markets, city streets, or festivals, stimulating creative problem-solving.

4. **Enhancing Visual Interest**

Ambiguous prompts can lead to more visually interesting and engaging images. The AI's interpretations of vague instructions often result in unique compositions and unexpected elements that capture attention.

Example:

- **Specific Prompt**: "A dog playing in a park"

- **Ambiguous Prompt**: "Joyful moments with a furry friend"

Analysis:

- The ambiguous prompt "Joyful moments with a furry friend" might result in various joyful scenes featuring pets in different environments and activities, enhancing visual interest.

Practical Examples of Ambiguity in Prompts

Example 1: Nature Scene

- **Specific Prompt**: "A waterfall cascading down rocks with a rainbow"

- **Ambiguous Prompt**: "A magical natural wonder"

Analysis:

- The ambiguous prompt "A magical natural wonder" allows the AI to explore different natural phenomena, such as waterfalls, forests, or mountains, creating diverse and enchanting images.

Example 2: Character Description

- **Specific Prompt**: "A young girl reading a book under a tree"

- **Ambiguous Prompt**: "A moment of discovery"

Analysis:

- The ambiguous prompt "A moment of discovery" can be interpreted in various ways, such as a child discovering nature, a scientist making a breakthrough, or an adventurer exploring new lands, resulting in a range of creative outputs.

Example 3: Urban Scene

- **Specific Prompt**: "A night market with colorful lights and street food vendors"

- **Ambiguous Prompt**: "A vibrant urban evening"

Analysis:

- The ambiguous prompt "A vibrant urban evening" allows the AI to depict different nighttime urban scenes, such as night markets, illuminated cityscapes, or lively streets, enhancing diversity and creativity.

Embracing ambiguity in prompt writing can significantly enhance creativity and lead to more diverse and innovative AI-generated images. By leaving room for interpretation, you foster innovation, encourage diverse outputs, stimulate creative problem-solving, and enhance visual interest. Using techniques such as open-ended descriptions, suggestive language, abstract concepts, and minimalist prompts, you can create more engaging and imaginative prompts that unlock new creative possibilities.

Balancing Specificity and Ambiguity

Balancing specificity and ambiguity in prompt writing is key to generating creative, diverse, and high-quality AI-generated images. While specificity provides clear guidance, ambiguity allows for exploration and innovation. Striking the right balance can enhance the richness and variety of the outputs.

The Importance of Balance

1. **Guiding the AI:**

o   Specificity ensures that the AI understands the core elements of the prompt, guiding it to produce relevant and coherent images.

2. **Encouraging Creativity**:

o   Ambiguity leaves room for the AI to interpret and experiment, fostering creativity and leading to unique and unexpected results.

3. **Enhancing Diversity**:

o   A balanced approach results in a diverse range of images, combining consistent core elements with varied interpretations and details.

Techniques for Balancing Specificity and Ambiguity

1. **Define Key Elements Clearly**:

o   Clearly specify the essential elements of the prompt to provide a strong foundation.

Example:

- **Specific Element**: "A medieval castle"

- **Ambiguous Elements**: "surrounded by a mysterious landscape"

Analysis:

- The specific element "A medieval castle" ensures the core subject is clear, while the ambiguous "surrounded by a mysterious landscape" allows for varied and creative interpretations of the surroundings.

2. **Use Suggestive Adjectives**:

o   Employ adjectives that suggest qualities without dictating exact details, providing room for interpretation.

Example:

- **Specific Element**: "A futuristic city"
- **Suggestive Adjectives**: "with shimmering skyscrapers and vibrant streets"

Analysis:

- "Shimmering" and "vibrant" suggest qualities but leave the specific appearance of the skyscrapers and streets open to interpretation, encouraging diverse outputs.

3. **Combine Concrete and Abstract Concepts**:

o   Mix concrete descriptions with abstract concepts to balance clarity and creativity.

Example:

- **Concrete Element**: "A warrior"
- **Abstract Concept**: "in a land of dreams"

Analysis:

- The concrete element "A warrior" provides a clear subject, while "in a land of dreams" introduces an abstract setting that can be visualized in many ways.

4. **Limit Detailed Descriptions**:

o   Provide detailed descriptions for key aspects but keep other parts open-ended to invite creativity.

Example:

- **Detailed Description**: "A lush forest with towering ancient trees"
- **Open-Ended Description**: "and an air of enchantment"

Analysis:

- The detailed description of the forest sets a clear scene, while "an air of enchantment" is open to interpretation, leading to creative and varied images.

Practical Examples

Example 1: Nature Scene

- **Balanced Prompt**: "A serene lake surrounded by towering pine trees, with hints of hidden magic"

Analysis:

- The specific elements ("serene lake," "towering pine trees") guide the AI, while "hints of hidden magic" introduces ambiguity, encouraging creative interpretations of the magical elements.

Example 2: Character Description

- **Balanced Prompt**: "A wise old wizard in a mystical land, with a mysterious aura"

Analysis:

- The specific elements ("wise old wizard," "mystical land") are clear, while "a mysterious aura" leaves room for creative depiction of the wizard's aura.

Example 3: Urban Scene

- **Balanced Prompt**: "A bustling city at night, with vibrant lights and an air of mystery"

Analysis:

- The specific elements ("bustling city at night," "vibrant lights") provide clear guidance, while "an air of mystery" introduces ambiguity, allowing for varied interpretations of the mysterious elements.

Balancing specificity and ambiguity in prompt writing enhances both the clarity and creativity of AI-generated images. By defining key elements clearly, using suggestive adjectives, combining concrete and abstract concepts, and limiting detailed descriptions to essential parts, you can guide the AI while leaving room for exploration and innovation. This balanced approach results in diverse, unique, and high-quality outputs, unlocking the full creative potential of AI.

Creative Prompt Examples

Creative prompt writing involves balancing specificity and ambiguity to inspire unique and innovative AI-generated images. Ambiguity can stimulate the AI's creativity, leading to diverse and unexpected outputs.

Creative Prompt Examples

Example 1: Nature Scene

- **Prompt**: "A hidden sanctuary in the heart of a mystical forest"

- **Analysis**: This prompt specifies a "hidden sanctuary" and a "mystical forest," guiding the AI to focus on a secluded and magical setting. The ambiguity lies in the nature of the sanctuary and the mystical elements, which can lead to diverse interpretations, such as enchanted glades, ancient ruins, or ethereal landscapes.

Example 2: Character Description

- **Prompt**: "A traveler from a distant land with secrets hidden in their eyes"

- **Analysis**: The prompt defines the subject as a "traveler from a distant land," providing a clear character foundation. The phrase "secrets hidden in their eyes" introduces ambiguity, allowing the AI to explore various interpretations of the character's background, experiences, and emotional depth.

Example 3: Urban Scene

- **Prompt**: "A bustling marketplace at twilight, filled with wonders and whispers"

- **Analysis**: This prompt sets the scene as a "bustling marketplace at twilight," ensuring the setting is clear. The terms "wonders and whispers" add an element of mystery and intrigue, prompting the AI to create a vibrant, dynamic market scene with magical or secretive undertones.

Example 4: Fantasy Landscape

- **Prompt**: "A realm where the skies change color with every breath of the wind"

- **Analysis**: The prompt establishes a fantastical setting with "skies that change color," which is specific yet open-ended. The phrase "with every breath of the wind" adds a poetic and ambiguous touch, encouraging the AI to generate imaginative and ever-changing sky landscapes.

Example 5: Artistic Scene

- **Prompt**: "An abstract representation of the essence of joy"

- **Analysis**: This prompt is intentionally vague, focusing on the abstract concept of "the essence of joy." It challenges the AI to interpret and visualize joy in various forms, such as through vibrant colors, dynamic shapes, or playful compositions, resulting in a wide array of artistic outputs.

Example 6: Historical Moment

- **Prompt**: "A moment frozen in time, capturing the triumphs and trials of an ancient civilization"

- **Analysis**: The prompt specifies "a moment frozen in time" and "an ancient civilization," providing a historical context. The terms "triumphs and trials" are ambiguous, allowing the AI to explore different events, emotions, and scenes from the civilization's history.

Example 7: Emotional Portrait

- **Prompt**: "A portrait of resilience, with a backdrop that tells a silent story of survival"

- **Analysis**: The prompt defines the subject as "a portrait of resilience," guiding the AI to focus on strength and determination. The phrase "a backdrop that tells a silent story of survival" introduces ambiguity, encouraging the AI to create backgrounds that subtly convey the narrative of overcoming adversity.

Example 8: Sci-Fi Environment

- **Prompt**: "A futuristic city where technology and nature coexist in harmony"

- **Analysis**: The prompt sets a clear setting with "a futuristic city," while the concept of "technology and nature coexist in harmony" adds an element of ambiguity. This encourages the AI to explore various ways technology and nature can be integrated, resulting in innovative and diverse urban landscapes.

Practical Tips for Crafting Creative Prompts

1. **Incorporate Abstract Concepts:**

- o Use abstract ideas that can be visualized in multiple ways, such as emotions, sensations, or philosophical themes.

- o **Example**: "A visual representation of serenity"

2. **Use Suggestive Language**:

- o Employ suggestive adjectives and verbs that imply qualities without defining specifics.

- o **Example**: "A landscape that feels like a dream"

3. **Balance Detail with Openness**:

- o Provide enough detail to guide the AI but leave key elements open to interpretation.

- o **Example**: "A warrior in a land where legends are born"

4. **Encourage Exploration**:

- o Frame prompts in a way that invites the AI to explore and experiment.

- o **Example**: "A cityscape that blends the past and future"

Embracing ambiguity in prompt writing can significantly enhance creativity and lead to more diverse and innovative AI-generated images. By balancing specificity with ambiguity, using abstract concepts, suggestive language, and open-ended descriptions, you can craft prompts that inspire unique and imaginative results. Experimenting with these techniques will unlock new creative possibilities and enrich your prompt writing practice.

Conclusion

Embracing ambiguity in prompt writing can significantly enhance creativity and lead to more diverse and innovative AI-generated images. Techniques such as open-ended descriptions, suggestive language, abstract concepts, and minimalist prompts encourage the AI to explore various interpretations and produce unique outputs. By balancing clarity with ambiguity, you can unlock new creative possibilities and achieve richer and more imaginative results.

Chapter 8: Iteration and Experimentation

Iteration and experimentation are essential practices in prompt writing for AI-generated images. These processes involve refining and tweaking prompts through multiple trials to achieve the best possible results. By experimenting with different wording, parameters, and styles, you can discover what works best for your specific creative goals.

The Importance of Iteration and Experimentation

1. **Refining Quality**:

o   Iteration allows you to progressively refine your prompts, improving the clarity, specificity, and creativity of the resulting images.

2. **Discovering What Works**:

o   Experimentation helps you understand how different elements of your prompt affect the AI's output, allowing you to identify the most effective strategies.

3. **Encouraging Creativity**:

o   Trying different approaches can lead to unexpected and innovative results, expanding your creative possibilities.

4. **Optimizing Results**:

o   Iterating on prompts enables you to optimize the generated images for specific criteria, such as style, detail, or mood.

Techniques for Iteration and Experimentation

1. **Varying Descriptive Elements**

Experiment with different descriptive elements to see how they affect the output. Change the adjectives, verbs, and nouns to explore various nuances and details.

Example:

- **Initial Prompt**: "A dark forest"

- **Iteration 1**: "A mysterious forest with towering trees"

- **Iteration 2**: "An eerie forest shrouded in mist"

Analysis:

- Each iteration introduces different descriptive elements, resulting in varied visual interpretations of the forest.

2. **Adjusting Parameters**

Use AI-specific parameters to refine the results. Adjusting parameters such as aspect ratio, chaos, quality, and stylize can significantly impact the generated images.

Example:

- **Initial Prompt**: "A serene beach at sunset"

- **Iteration 1**: "A serene beach at sunset --ar 16:9"

- **Iteration 2**: "A serene beach at sunset --chaos 30"

- **Iteration 3**: "A serene beach at sunset --q 2"

Analysis:

- Different parameters affect the composition, creativity, and detail of the images, offering a range of outputs from the same basic prompt.

3. **Exploring Different Styles**

Experiment with various styles by adjusting the tone and focus of your prompts. This can lead to discovering new creative directions and aesthetics.

Example:

- **Initial Prompt**: "A castle on a hill"

- **Iteration 1**: "A medieval castle on a misty hill"

- **Iteration 2**: "A futuristic castle on a high-tech hill"

- **Iteration 3**: "A whimsical castle on a candy hill"

Analysis:

- Each iteration shifts the style and theme, producing diverse and imaginative interpretations of the castle scene.

4. **Using Synonyms**

Experiment with synonyms to add variety and richness to your prompts. Different words can evoke different imagery and emotions.

Example:

- **Initial Prompt**: "A beautiful garden"

- **Iteration 1**: "A charming garden"

- **Iteration 2**: "A picturesque garden"

- **Iteration 3**: "A delightful garden"

Analysis:

- Each synonym adds a unique nuance, leading to varied visual outputs while maintaining the core concept of a garden.

Practical Examples of Iteration and Experimentation

Example 1: Character Description

- **Initial Prompt**: "A wise old wizard"

- **Iteration 1**: "A wise old wizard with a long white beard and a sparkling staff"

- **Iteration 2**: "A wise old wizard in a mystical forest, surrounded by glowing runes"

- **Iteration 3**: "A wise old wizard casting a powerful spell under a starry sky"

Analysis:

- Iterations add details and context, enriching the character's depiction and exploring different scenarios.

Example 2: Urban Scene

- **Initial Prompt**: "A busy street at night"

- **Iteration 1**: "A busy street at night with neon lights and bustling crowds"

- **Iteration 2**: "A busy street at night with street performers and food stalls"

- **Iteration 3**: "A busy street at night with glowing skyscrapers and passing cars"

Analysis:

- Each iteration focuses on different elements of the urban scene, resulting in varied and dynamic images.

Example 3: Fantasy Landscape

- **Initial Prompt**: "A magical forest"

- **Iteration 1**: "A magical forest with glowing mushrooms and sparkling streams"

- **Iteration 2**: "A magical forest with enchanted creatures and hidden paths"

- **Iteration 3**: "A magical forest with ancient trees and a shimmering lake"

Analysis:

- Iterations explore different aspects of the magical forest, enhancing the richness and diversity of the generated images.

The Importance of Iteration in Prompt Writing

Iteration is a critical component of prompt writing for AI-generated images. By refining and tweaking prompts through multiple iterations, you can progressively enhance the clarity, creativity, and effectiveness of your prompts. This process allows you to learn from each output, understand how different elements impact the result, and optimize your prompts for the best possible outcomes.

The Importance of Iteration

1. **Improving Clarity and Specificity**

- Iteration helps refine the language of your prompts, making them clearer and more specific. Each iteration allows you to identify ambiguities or vague terms and replace them with precise descriptions.

2. **Enhancing Creativity**

- By experimenting with different wordings and structures, you can discover new ways to stimulate the AI's creativity. Iteration encourages you to explore various angles and perspectives, leading to more innovative outputs.

3. **Optimizing Results**

o   Through repeated trials, you can identify which elements of your prompt are most effective in achieving your desired outcome. This optimization process ensures that your prompts consistently produce high-quality images.

4. **Learning and Adapting**

o   Iteration is a learning process. Each generated image provides feedback on how the AI interprets your prompt, helping you adapt your writing to better guide the AI.

Examples of Iteration in Prompt Writing

Example 1: Nature Scene

- **Initial Prompt**: "A peaceful forest"

- **Iteration 1**: "A peaceful forest with tall trees and a clear stream"

- **Iteration 2**: "A tranquil forest with towering pines and a crystal-clear stream running through it"

- **Iteration 3**: "A serene forest with majestic pine trees, a babbling brook, and dappled sunlight filtering through the canopy"

Analysis:

- Each iteration adds more detail and specificity, enhancing the visual richness and clarity of the prompt. The final iteration provides a vivid and immersive description that guides the AI to generate a more detailed and appealing image.

Example 2: Character Description

- **Initial Prompt**: "A brave knight"

- **Iteration 1**: "A brave knight in shining armor"

- **Iteration 2**: "A courageous knight in gleaming armor, holding a sword"

- **Iteration 3**: "A valiant knight in polished silver armor, brandishing a sword, with a determined expression and a golden crest on his chestplate"

Analysis:

- The iterations progressively add more specific details about the knight's appearance, equipment, and demeanor. The final prompt provides a comprehensive description that helps the AI generate a more accurate and compelling character image.

Example 3: Urban Scene

- **Initial Prompt**: "A busy street"

- **Iteration 1**: "A busy street with people walking"

- **Iteration 2**: "A bustling street with pedestrians, street vendors, and colorful storefronts"

- **Iteration 3**: "A vibrant city street teeming with pedestrians, street vendors selling various goods, and colorful storefronts under a clear blue sky"

Analysis:

- Each iteration enhances the scene's detail and atmosphere, making the final prompt more engaging and visually interesting. The increased specificity helps the AI generate a more lively and detailed urban scene.

Practical Tips for Effective Iteration

1. **Start with a Basic Prompt**

   o   Begin with a simple, clear description. Identify the core elements you want to include.

2. **Add Detail Gradually**

   o   With each iteration, add more details and refine the language. Focus on enhancing the visual and sensory elements.

3. **Evaluate and Adjust**

   o   After each iteration, evaluate the generated image. Identify which parts of the prompt were most effective and which need further refinement.

4. **Experiment with Variations**

   o   Try different synonyms, adjectives, and structures. Experiment with various styles and tones to see how they affect the output.

5. **Incorporate Feedback**

   o   Use feedback from the generated images to guide your iterations. Learn from each result and adapt your prompts accordingly.

Iteration is essential for optimizing prompt writing for AI-generated images. By progressively refining your prompts through multiple iterations, you can improve clarity, enhance creativity, optimize results, and learn from each output. This iterative process ensures that your prompts consistently produce high-quality and visually appealing images. Experimenting with different wordings, structures, and details helps unlock new creative possibilities and achieve the best possible.

How to Experiment with Different Variations

Experimenting with different variations in prompt writing is key to discovering the most effective and creative ways to guide AI-generated images. By trying out multiple approaches, you can find the best combination of words, phrases, and structures to achieve your desired outcomes.

Techniques for Experimenting with Variations

1. Synonym Substitution

Using synonyms can change the tone, style, and detail of your prompts, leading to varied interpretations by the AI.

Example:

- **Initial Prompt**: "A beautiful garden"

- **Variation 1**: "A picturesque garden"

- **Variation 2**: "A charming garden"

- **Variation 3**: "A delightful garden"

Analysis:

- Each synonym adds a unique nuance, potentially leading to different visual outputs that highlight various aspects of beauty in a garden.

2. Changing Adjectives and Adverbs

Experimenting with different adjectives and adverbs can significantly alter the imagery and mood of the generated images.

Example:

- **Initial Prompt**: "A fast car"

- **Variation 1**: "A sleek, fast car"

- **Variation 2**: "A roaring, high-speed car"

- **Variation 3**: "A futuristic, lightning-quick car"

Analysis:

- Different adjectives and adverbs create distinct images, from a modern and stylish car to one that emphasizes speed and power.

3. **Modifying Context and Setting**

Changing the context or setting can provide new dimensions to the subject, enriching the narrative and visual diversity.

Example:

- **Initial Prompt**: "A lion in the jungle"

- **Variation 1**: "A lion on the savanna"

- **Variation 2**: "A lion resting in a dense forest"

- **Variation 3**: "A lion standing majestically on a rocky cliff"

Analysis:

- Each setting variation offers a different backdrop and atmosphere, influencing how the AI portrays the lion and its environment.

4. **Incorporating Different Actions**

Varying the actions performed by subjects can lead to dynamic and engaging images.

Example:

- **Initial Prompt**: "A girl reading a book"
- **Variation 1**: "A girl reading a book under a tree"
- **Variation 2**: "A girl reading a book by the fireplace"
- **Variation 3**: "A girl reading a book on a sunny beach"

Analysis:

- Different actions and settings provide varied scenes, each with unique elements that contribute to the overall image.

5. **Exploring Emotional Tones**

Changing the emotional tone of the prompt can affect the mood and feeling of the generated images.

Example:

- **Initial Prompt**: "A happy family"
- **Variation 1**: "A joyful family celebrating"
- **Variation 2**: "A peaceful family enjoying a quiet evening"
- **Variation 3**: "A loving family sharing a meal"

Analysis:

- Each emotional tone sets a different atmosphere, leading the AI to generate images that evoke specific feelings and scenarios.

Practical Examples of Experimenting with Variations

Example 1: Nature Scene

- **Initial Prompt**: "A serene lake"
- **Variation 1**: "A tranquil lake at sunrise"
- **Variation 2**: "A peaceful lake surrounded by mountains"

- **Variation 3**: "A calm lake with crystal-clear water and reflections of the sky"

Analysis:

- Variations in time of day, surrounding environment, and specific attributes of the lake create diverse visual outputs, each emphasizing different aspects of serenity.

Example 2: Character Description

- **Initial Prompt**: "A brave warrior"

- **Variation 1**: "A fearless warrior in battle"

- **Variation 2**: "A determined warrior standing guard"

- **Variation 3**: "A heroic warrior leading an army"

Analysis:

- Each variation highlights different facets of bravery and context, leading to varied portrayals of the warrior's character and setting.

Example 3: Urban Scene

- **Initial Prompt**: "A bustling city street"

- **Variation 1**: "A bustling city street at dusk"

- **Variation 2**: "A busy city street with neon lights"

- **Variation 3**: "A vibrant city street during a festival"

Analysis:

- Changes in time of day, lighting, and events transform the scene, providing a range of dynamic and engaging urban images.

Experimenting with different variations in prompt writing is essential for discovering the most effective ways to guide AI-generated images. Techniques such as synonym substitution, changing adjectives and adverbs, modifying context and setting, incorporating different actions, and exploring emotional tones can significantly enhance the diversity and creativity of the outputs. By trying out multiple approaches and learning from each iteration, you can refine your prompts and achieve the best possible results in your creative projects.

Case Studies of Iterative Prompt Refinement

Iterative prompt refinement is a process of progressively improving prompt quality through multiple iterations. Each iteration involves analyzing the AI-generated output, identifying areas for improvement, and modifying the prompt accordingly. This approach helps in optimizing prompts to achieve the best possible results.

Case Study 1: Creating a Nature Scene

Initial Prompt: "A beautiful forest"

Iteration 1:

- **Prompt**: "A dense, beautiful forest"

- **Analysis**: The generated image includes a forest but lacks specific features that enhance its beauty.

- **Refinement**: Add more descriptive elements.

Iteration 2:

- **Prompt**: "A dense, beautiful forest with tall, ancient trees"

- **Analysis**: The image now has tall trees, but it still feels generic.

- **Refinement**: Introduce additional sensory details.

Iteration 3:

- **Prompt**: "A dense, beautiful forest with tall, ancient trees and a crystal-clear stream flowing through it"

- **Analysis**: The addition of the stream improves the image, but it needs more elements to enhance the atmosphere.

- **Refinement**: Add elements that evoke sensory experiences.

Final Prompt:

- **Prompt**: "A dense, beautiful forest with tall, ancient trees, a crystal-clear stream flowing through it, and the soft sound of birds singing"

- **Analysis**: The final image is rich and atmospheric, capturing the essence of a beautiful forest.

Case Study 2: Depicting a Character

Initial Prompt: "A brave knight"

Iteration 1:

- **Prompt**: "A brave knight in shining armor"

- **Analysis**: The image includes a knight, but it lacks context and emotional depth.

- **Refinement**: Add contextual details to provide a setting.

Iteration 2:

- **Prompt**: "A brave knight in shining armor standing in a battlefield"

- **Analysis**: The battlefield adds context, but the image still feels static.

- **Refinement**: Introduce action to add dynamism.

Iteration 3:

- **Prompt**: "A brave knight in shining armor standing in a battlefield, raising his sword triumphantly"

- **Analysis**: The action enhances the image, but it needs more detail to convey emotion.

- **Refinement**: Include elements that highlight the knight's bravery.

Final Prompt:

- **Prompt**: "A brave knight in shining armor standing in a battlefield, raising his sword triumphantly, with a determined look in his eyes and the sunset casting a golden glow"

- **Analysis**: The final image is dynamic and emotionally powerful, capturing the knight's bravery and determination.

Case Study 3: Urban Scene

Initial Prompt: "A busy city street"

Iteration 1:

- **Prompt**: "A busy city street at night"

- **Analysis**: The night setting adds interest, but the image lacks vibrancy.

- **Refinement**: Add more specific elements to enhance the scene's energy.

Iteration 2:

- **Prompt**: "A busy city street at night with neon lights and crowds of people"

- **Analysis**: The neon lights and crowds improve the scene, but it still feels incomplete.

- **Refinement**: Introduce additional elements that enhance the urban atmosphere.

Iteration 3:

- **Prompt**: "A busy city street at night with neon lights, crowds of people, street vendors, and colorful billboards"

- **Analysis**: The added elements create a vibrant scene, but it could benefit from more detail.

- **Refinement**: Include sensory details to make the scene more immersive.

Final Prompt:

- **Prompt**: "A busy city street at night with neon lights, crowds of people, street vendors, colorful billboards, and the aroma of street food wafting through the air"

- **Analysis**: The final image is rich and vibrant, capturing the bustling energy and sensory experiences of a busy city street at night.

Iterative prompt refinement is a powerful technique for optimizing AI-generated images. By progressively enhancing the prompt through multiple iterations, you can achieve clearer, more detailed, and more creative results. These case studies demonstrate how careful analysis and targeted refinements can transform simple prompts into rich, engaging, and visually compelling images. Experimentation and iteration are key to unlocking the full potential of AI in creative projects.

Conclusion

Iteration and experimentation are vital techniques in prompt writing for AI-generated images. By varying descriptive elements, adjusting parameters, exploring different styles, and using synonyms, you can refine your prompts and achieve more creative and high-quality results. These practices encourage continuous improvement and innovation, enabling you to discover new creative possibilities and optimize the generated images to meet your specific goals.

Chapter 9: Multi-Prompt Techniques

Multi-prompt techniques involve using multiple prompts to generate more complex and detailed AI-generated images. By combining different prompts, you can provide the AI with a broader context and richer information, leading to more nuanced and intricate outputs. This approach allows for greater creative control and flexibility, enabling you to craft images that meet specific creative goals.

The Benefits of Multi-Prompt Techniques

1. **Enhanced Detail and Depth**:

o   Combining prompts allows for the inclusion of more details and layers, resulting in richer and more intricate images.

2. **Increased Contextual Relevance**:

o   Multiple prompts can provide different aspects of a scene or subject, ensuring that the AI-generated image is more contextually relevant and comprehensive.

3. **Greater Creative Flexibility**:

o   Multi-prompt techniques offer flexibility in directing the AI, allowing for more complex and creative compositions.

4. **Improved Accuracy**:

o   By addressing different elements separately, multi-prompt techniques can improve the accuracy of the generated images, ensuring that all desired aspects are captured effectively.

Techniques for Multi-Prompt Writing

1. **Sequential Prompts**

Use a series of prompts to build up the scene step by step, adding layers of detail and complexity.

Example:

- **Prompt 1**: "A medieval castle on a hill"

- **Prompt 2**: "Surrounded by lush green forests"

- **Prompt 3**: "With a sparkling river flowing at the base of the hill"

- **Combined Description**: "A medieval castle on a hill, surrounded by lush green forests, with a sparkling river flowing at the base of the hill."

Analysis:

- Each prompt adds a new layer of detail, resulting in a comprehensive and detailed scene.

2. **Parallel Prompts**

Use multiple prompts to describe different elements of the same scene or subject simultaneously.

Example:

- **Prompt 1**: "A bustling marketplace at twilight"

- **Prompt 2**: "Street vendors selling exotic fruits and spices"

- **Prompt 3**: "Colorful lanterns illuminating the stalls"

- **Combined Description**: "A bustling marketplace at twilight, with street vendors selling exotic fruits and spices, and colorful lanterns illuminating the stalls."

Analysis:

- Parallel prompts address different aspects of the scene, providing a well-rounded and vibrant image.

3. **Contrasting Prompts**

Use prompts that highlight contrasts or juxtapositions to create dynamic and visually interesting images.

Example:

- **Prompt 1**: "A modern city skyline"

- **Prompt 2**: "Against an ancient, crumbling castle"

- **Combined Description**: "A modern city skyline against an ancient, crumbling castle."

Analysis:

- The contrast between the modern skyline and the ancient castle creates a striking and thought-provoking image.

4. **Complementary Prompts**

Use prompts that complement each other to enhance the overall coherence and harmony of the image.

Example:

- **Prompt 1**: "A serene lake"

- **Prompt 2**: "Reflecting the colorful autumn foliage"

- **Combined Description**: "A serene lake reflecting the colorful autumn foliage."

Analysis:

- Complementary prompts work together to create a harmonious and visually pleasing scene.

Practical Examples of Multi-Prompt Techniques

Example 1: Nature Scene

- **Prompt 1**: "A tranquil forest"

- **Prompt 2**: "With sunlight filtering through the leaves"

- **Prompt 3**: "And a clear stream flowing through"

- **Combined Description**: "A tranquil forest with sunlight filtering through the leaves and a clear stream flowing through."

Analysis:

- The combined prompts create a detailed and serene forest scene, capturing multiple elements that enhance the overall image.

Example 2: Character Description

- **Prompt 1**: "A fierce warrior"

- **Prompt 2**: "With a scarred face and determined eyes"

- **Prompt 3**: "Wielding a glowing sword"

- **Combined Description**: "A fierce warrior with a scarred face and determined eyes, wielding a glowing sword."

Analysis:

- Each prompt adds specific details about the warrior's appearance and equipment, resulting in a vivid and dynamic character image.

Example 3: Urban Scene

- **Prompt 1**: "A busy city street"

- **Prompt 2**: "Filled with honking cars and rushing pedestrians"

- **Prompt 3**: "Bright neon signs lighting up the night"

- **Combined Description**: "A busy city street filled with honking cars and rushing pedestrians, with bright neon signs lighting up the night."

Analysis:

- The combined prompts capture the energy and vibrancy of a busy city street, providing a comprehensive and lively urban scene.

What are Multi-Prompts?

Multi-prompts are a powerful technique used in prompt writing for AI-generated images. This method involves using multiple prompts to provide detailed and layered instructions to the AI. By breaking down a complex scene or concept into several simpler prompts, you can achieve greater specificity, creativity, and depth in the resulting images. This section explores the concept of multi-prompts, their benefits, and practical examples to illustrate their application.

Understanding Multi-Prompts

Multi-prompts involve crafting several interrelated prompts that work together to create a cohesive and detailed image. Instead of relying on a single, complex prompt, multi-prompts allow you to focus on different aspects of the scene or subject, providing the AI with comprehensive guidance. This technique can enhance the overall quality and creativity of the generated images by ensuring that all important elements are included and well-defined.

Benefits of Multi-Prompts

1. **Enhanced Detail and Depth**:

o   By dividing the scene into multiple prompts, you can include more details and layers, resulting in richer and more intricate images.

2. **Increased Specificity**:

o   Multi-prompts allow you to address specific aspects of the scene separately, ensuring that each element is clearly defined and accurately represented.

3. **Improved Creativity**:

o   Breaking down a complex idea into simpler components encourages creative exploration and experimentation, leading to more innovative and varied outputs.

4. **Greater Control**:

o   Using multiple prompts gives you more control over the final image, allowing you to guide the AI through each step of the creation process.

Types of Multi-Prompt Techniques

1. **Sequential Prompts**:

o   Using a series of prompts to build up the scene step by step, adding layers of detail and complexity.

2. **Parallel Prompts**:

o   Providing multiple prompts that describe different elements of the same scene or subject simultaneously.

3. **Contrasting Prompts**:

o   Using prompts that highlight contrasts or juxtapositions to create dynamic and visually interesting images.

4. **Complementary Prompts**:

o Combining prompts that complement each other to enhance the overall coherence and harmony of the image.

Examples of Multi-Prompts

Example 1: Creating a Nature Scene

Sequential Prompts:

- **Prompt 1**: "A peaceful meadow"

- **Prompt 2**: "With wildflowers in full bloom"

- **Prompt 3**: "And butterflies fluttering around"

Combined Description: "A peaceful meadow, with wildflowers in full bloom and butterflies fluttering around."

Analysis: Each prompt adds a new layer of detail, resulting in a comprehensive and vibrant meadow scene.

Example 2: Depicting a Character

Parallel Prompts:

- **Prompt 1**: "A wise old wizard"

- **Prompt 2**: "With a long, flowing beard"

- **Prompt 3**: "Holding a staff topped with a glowing crystal"

Combined Description: "A wise old wizard, with a long, flowing beard, holding a staff topped with a glowing crystal."

Analysis: Parallel prompts address different aspects of the wizard's appearance and equipment, creating a detailed and dynamic character image.

Example 3: Urban Scene

Contrasting Prompts:

- **Prompt 1**: "A modern city skyline"

- **Prompt 2**: "With an ancient temple in the foreground"

Combined Description: "A modern city skyline, with an ancient temple in the foreground."

Analysis: The contrast between the modern skyline and the ancient temple creates a visually striking and thought-provoking image.

Example 4: Fantasy Landscape

Complementary Prompts:

- **Prompt 1**: "A serene lake"

- **Prompt 2**: "Reflecting the colorful autumn foliage"

- **Prompt 3**: "With a majestic mountain range in the background"

Combined Description: "A serene lake reflecting the colorful autumn foliage, with a majestic mountain range in the background."

Analysis: Complementary prompts work together to create a harmonious and visually pleasing landscape scene.

Practical Tips for Crafting Multi-Prompts

1. **Identify Key Elements:**

   o Break down the scene or subject into its essential components, and create separate prompts for each element.

2. **Use Descriptive Language:**

   o Ensure that each prompt is detailed and descriptive, providing clear guidance to the AI.

3. **Maintain Coherence**:

o   Ensure that the prompts are interrelated and work together to create a cohesive image.

4. **Experiment with Different Techniques**:

o   Try different types of multi-prompts (sequential, parallel, contrasting, complementary) to see which approach works best for your specific creative goals.

Multi-prompts are a versatile and powerful technique for enhancing the detail, depth, and creativity of AI-generated images. By using sequential, parallel, contrasting, and complementary prompts, you can provide comprehensive guidance to the AI, resulting in more nuanced, contextually relevant, and visually interesting images. Experimenting with different multi-prompt techniques allows for greater creative flexibility and improved accuracy, helping you achieve your specific creative goals more effectively.

Breaking Down Complex Images into Simpler Prompts

Creating complex and detailed AI-generated images can be challenging with a single prompt. Breaking down complex images into simpler, more manageable prompts is an effective technique to achieve nuanced and comprehensive results. This approach involves identifying the key elements of the desired image and crafting individual prompts for each element.

The Process of Breaking Down Complex Images

1. **Identify Key Elements**:

o   Determine the main components of the image. These could include the setting, main subjects, background details, and specific actions or features.

2. **Create Individual Prompts**:

o   Write separate prompts for each key element, focusing on providing clear and detailed descriptions.

3. **Combine Prompts**:

o   Integrate the individual prompts to form a comprehensive description that guides the AI to generate a cohesive and detailed image.

4. **Iterate and Refine**:

o   Refine each prompt through iteration, ensuring that all elements work together harmoniously.

Benefits of Breaking Down Complex Images

1. **Enhanced Detail and Precision**:

o   By focusing on individual elements, you can provide more detailed and precise descriptions, resulting in a richer image.

2. **Improved Clarity**:

o   Breaking down the scene into simpler prompts helps avoid ambiguity and ensures that each element is clearly defined.

3. **Greater Flexibility**:

o   This approach allows for more flexibility in modifying and refining specific parts of the image without affecting the entire scene.

4. **Creative Exploration**:

o   Experimenting with different combinations of prompts can lead to innovative and unexpected results.

Practical Examples of Breaking Down Complex Images

Example 1: Creating a Detailed Urban Scene

Complex Image:

- A vibrant city street at night with bustling crowds, neon lights, street performers, and food vendors.

Breaking Down the Image:

Element 1: Setting

- **Prompt**: "A vibrant city street at night"

Element 2: Main Subjects

- **Prompt**: "Bustling crowds of people"

Element 3: Lighting

- **Prompt**: "Neon lights illuminating the scene"

Element 4: Activities

- **Prompt**: "Street performers entertaining passersby"

Element 5: Additional Features

- **Prompt**: "Food vendors selling a variety of snacks"

Combined Description:

- "A vibrant city street at night, with bustling crowds of people, neon lights illuminating the scene, street performers entertaining passersby, and food vendors selling a variety of snacks."

Example 2: Depicting a Fantasy Landscape

Complex Image:

- A mystical forest with towering trees, magical creatures, glowing plants, and a crystal-clear stream.

Breaking Down the Image:

Element 1: Setting

- **Prompt**: "A mystical forest with towering trees"

Element 2: Main Subjects

- **Prompt**: "Magical creatures roaming the forest"

Element 3: Lighting

- **Prompt**: "Glowing plants illuminating the area"

Element 4: Additional Features

- **Prompt**: "A crystal-clear stream flowing through the forest"

Combined Description:

- "A mystical forest with towering trees, magical creatures roaming the forest, glowing plants illuminating the area, and a crystal-clear stream flowing through the forest."

Example 3: Illustrating a Historical Event

Complex Image:

- A grand medieval battle with knights in armor, horses charging, banners flying, and a castle in the background.

Breaking Down the Image:

Element 1: Setting

- **Prompt**: "A grand medieval battlefield"

Element 2: Main Subjects

- **Prompt**: "Knights in shining armor"

Element 3: Action

- **Prompt**: "Horses charging into battle"

Element 4: Additional Features

- **Prompt**: "Banners flying in the wind"

Element 5: Background

- **Prompt**: "A castle standing tall in the background"

Combined Description:

- "A grand medieval battlefield, with knights in shining armor, horses charging into battle, banners flying in the wind, and a castle standing tall in the background."

Tips for Effective Multi-Prompt Writing

1. **Prioritize Key Elements**:

   o Focus on the most important aspects of the scene first, ensuring that the core elements are well-defined.

2. **Be Descriptive and Specific**:

   o Use clear and detailed language to describe each element, providing the AI with precise guidance.

3. **Maintain Coherence**:

   o Ensure that the individual prompts work together harmoniously to form a cohesive image.

4. **Experiment and Refine**:

   o Continuously iterate and refine each prompt based on the generated images, adjusting as necessary to achieve the desired result.

Breaking down complex images into simpler prompts is an effective technique for creating detailed, precise, and creative AI-generated images. By identifying key elements, crafting individual prompts, and combining them into a comprehensive description, you can provide the AI with clear and detailed instructions. This approach enhances the quality and creativity of the generated images, allowing for greater flexibility and innovation in prompt writing. Experimenting with different combinations and refining each prompt ensures that the final image is rich, cohesive, and visually compelling.

Practical Examples of Multi-Prompts

Multi-prompt techniques involve using multiple, interrelated prompts to create more detailed, nuanced, and contextually rich AI-generated images. This approach allows you to break down complex scenes or concepts into simpler, more manageable components, ensuring that each element is well-defined and contributes to the overall image.

Practical Examples of Multi-Prompts

Example 1: Crafting a Detailed Nature Scene

Complex Scene: A tranquil forest glade with wildlife, flowers, and a sparkling stream.

Breaking Down the Scene:

1. **Setting:**

   o **Prompt**: "A tranquil forest glade"

   o **Description**: Establishes the main setting, providing a calm and serene atmosphere.

2. **Wildlife:**

   o **Prompt**: "Deer grazing peacefully"

o **Description**: Introduces the presence of wildlife, adding life and movement to the scene.

3. **Flora**:

o **Prompt**: "Wildflowers in full bloom"

o **Description**: Adds color and detail to the environment, enhancing the natural beauty.

4. **Water Feature**:

o **Prompt**: "A sparkling stream flowing gently"

o **Description**: Complements the tranquil setting with a dynamic element, reflecting light and adding sound.

Combined Description:

- "A tranquil forest glade, with deer grazing peacefully, wildflowers in full bloom, and a sparkling stream flowing gently."

Analysis:

- This multi-prompt approach breaks down the scene into key elements, ensuring each aspect is vividly depicted and contributes to the overall tranquility and beauty of the image.

Example 2: Depicting a Bustling Market

Complex Scene: A vibrant market at dusk with various vendors, customers, and atmospheric lighting.

Breaking Down the Scene:

1. **Setting**:

o **Prompt**: "A bustling market at dusk"

- o **Description**: Sets the overall scene with a specific time of day, adding a unique lighting effect.

2. **Vendors**:

- o **Prompt**: "Vendors selling exotic fruits and spices"

- o **Description**: Adds detail and specificity, highlighting the diversity of goods available.

3. **Customers**:

- o **Prompt**: "Customers haggling and buying goods"

- o **Description**: Introduces dynamic human interaction, making the scene lively and engaging.

4. **Lighting**:

- o **Prompt**: "Lanterns and string lights illuminating the stalls"

- o **Description**: Enhances the atmosphere with warm, ambient lighting, creating a cozy and inviting environment.

Combined Description:

- • "A bustling market at dusk, with vendors selling exotic fruits and spices, customers haggling and buying goods, and lanterns and string lights illuminating the stalls."

Analysis:

- • This approach ensures that each aspect of the market scene is well-represented, creating a vivid and dynamic image full of activity and atmosphere.

Example 3: Illustrating a Fantasy Battle

Complex Scene: A grand battle between knights and dragons in a mystical land.

Breaking Down the Scene:

1. **Setting**:

o **Prompt**: "A mystical battlefield"

o **Description**: Establishes the fantasy setting, hinting at magical elements.

2. **Main Action**:

o **Prompt**: "Knights in shining armor clashing with dragons"

o **Description**: Describes the central conflict, highlighting the key characters and action.

3. **Atmospheric Details**:

o **Prompt**: "Enchanted forests and glowing runes in the background"

o **Description**: Adds depth and detail to the environment, enhancing the fantasy theme.

4. **Visual Effects**:

o **Prompt**: "Fire and lightning illuminating the sky"

o **Description**: Introduces dynamic and dramatic visual elements, making the scene more intense and engaging.

Combined Description:

• "A mystical battlefield, with knights in shining armor clashing with dragons, enchanted forests and glowing runes in the background, and fire and lightning illuminating the sky."

Analysis:

- Each prompt adds a specific layer of detail, ensuring that the final image is rich, dynamic, and immersive, capturing the epic scale and fantasy elements of the battle.

Tips for Creating Effective Multi-Prompts

1. **Focus on Key Elements**:

o Identify the main components of your scene and create individual prompts for each one, ensuring that all important aspects are covered.

2. **Be Descriptive and Specific**:

o Use detailed and specific language to provide clear guidance for each prompt, helping the AI generate accurate and vivid images.

3. **Ensure Coherence**:

o Make sure that the individual prompts are interrelated and work together to form a cohesive and harmonious image.

4. **Experiment and Iterate**:

o Try different combinations and iterations of prompts to see what works best, refining your approach based on the generated images.

Multi-prompt techniques are a powerful tool for enhancing the detail, depth, and creativity of AI-generated images. By breaking down complex scenes into simpler, interrelated prompts, you can provide comprehensive guidance to the AI, resulting in more nuanced and contextually rich images. This approach allows for greater control, flexibility, and innovation in prompt writing, helping you achieve your specific creative goals more effectively.

Conclusion

Multi-prompt techniques are powerful tools for enhancing the detail, depth, and creativity of AI-generated images. By combining sequential, parallel, contrasting, and complementary prompts, you can guide the AI to produce more nuanced, contextually relevant, and visually interesting images. Experimenting with different multi-prompt techniques allows for greater creative flexibility and improved accuracy, helping you achieve your specific creative goals more effectively.

Chapter 10: Advanced Techniques

Advanced prompt writing techniques involve leveraging a deeper understanding of language, context, and the capabilities of AI to create sophisticated, nuanced, and highly detailed images. These techniques go beyond basic prompt writing, incorporating elements such as context layering, thematic consistency, emotional tone, and stylistic direction.

Context Layering

Context layering involves providing the AI with background information or a sequence of related prompts that build upon each other to create a comprehensive and detailed image.

Example:

- **Initial Prompt**: "A grand library"

- **Layer 1**: "Rows of ancient, leather-bound books"

- **Layer 2**: "Golden chandeliers casting a warm glow"

- **Layer 3**: "An elderly librarian reading at a mahogany desk"

Combined Description: "A grand library with rows of ancient, leather-bound books, golden chandeliers casting a warm glow, and an elderly librarian reading at a mahogany desk."

Analysis:

- Each layer adds depth and detail, creating a rich and immersive scene.

Thematic Consistency

Maintaining thematic consistency ensures that all elements of the prompt align with a central theme, creating a cohesive and harmonious image.

Example:

- **Theme**: Gothic Fantasy

- **Setting Prompt**: "An eerie, mist-covered graveyard"

- **Character Prompt**: "A brooding vampire with a flowing black cloak"

- **Atmospheric Detail Prompt**: "Bats flying under a crescent moon"

- **Action Prompt**: "The vampire standing beside an ancient, crumbling tombstone"

Combined Description: "An eerie, mist-covered graveyard with a brooding vampire in a flowing black cloak, bats flying under a crescent moon, and the vampire standing beside an ancient, crumbling tombstone."

Analysis:

- Each element adheres to the Gothic fantasy theme, ensuring a consistent and immersive atmosphere.

Emotional Tone

Incorporating emotional tone into prompts can guide the AI to generate images that evoke specific feelings or moods.

Example:

- **Emotion**: Melancholy

- **Setting Prompt**: "A desolate, windswept beach at dusk"

- **Character Prompt**: "A solitary figure standing at the water's edge"

- **Atmospheric Detail Prompt**: "Gray clouds rolling in over the horizon"

- **Action Prompt**: "The figure gazing out at the sea, lost in thought"

Combined Description: "A desolate, windswept beach at dusk with a solitary figure standing at the water's edge, gray clouds rolling in over the horizon, and the figure gazing out at the sea, lost in thought."

Analysis:

- The prompts collectively evoke a sense of melancholy, with each element reinforcing the emotional tone.

Stylistic Direction

Providing stylistic direction can help achieve a specific artistic style or aesthetic in the generated images.

Example:

- **Style**: Art Deco

- **Architecture Prompt**: "An elegant skyscraper with geometric designs"

- **Interior Detail Prompt**: "Luxurious furnishings with bold, symmetrical patterns"

- **Color Scheme Prompt**: "A palette of gold, black, and deep green"

- **Lighting Prompt**: "Soft, ambient lighting highlighting the intricate details"

Combined Description: "An elegant skyscraper with geometric designs, luxurious furnishings with bold, symmetrical patterns, a palette of gold, black, and deep green, and soft, ambient lighting highlighting the intricate details."

Analysis:

- Each prompt is crafted to reflect the Art Deco style, ensuring that the final image adheres to this aesthetic.

Symbolism and Metaphor

Using symbolism and metaphor can add layers of meaning to the image, making it more thought-provoking and visually rich.

Example:

- **Symbolism**: Transformation

- **Setting Prompt**: "A chrysalis hanging from a branch"

- **Character Prompt**: "A butterfly emerging from the chrysalis"

- **Atmospheric Detail Prompt**: "Morning light filtering through the leaves"

- **Action Prompt**: "The butterfly spreading its wings for the first time"

Combined Description: "A chrysalis hanging from a branch with a butterfly emerging, morning light filtering through the leaves, and the butterfly spreading its wings for the first time."

Analysis:

- The prompts use the butterfly's transformation as a metaphor for change and growth, adding symbolic depth to the image.

Practical Examples of Advanced Techniques

Example 1: Sci-Fi Landscape

Context Layering:

- **Setting Prompt**: "A futuristic city on a distant planet"

- **Technology Detail Prompt**: "Hover cars zipping through neon-lit streets"

- **Atmospheric Detail Prompt**: "Twin suns setting in the purple sky"

- **Character Prompt**: "Aliens and humans coexisting peacefully"

Combined Description: "A futuristic city on a distant planet with hover cars zipping through neon-lit streets, twin suns setting in the purple sky, and aliens and humans coexisting peacefully."

Example 2: Historical Scene

Thematic Consistency:

- **Theme**: Renaissance

- **Setting Prompt**: "A bustling Italian marketplace"

- **Character Prompt**: "Artists sketching in the square"

- **Atmospheric Detail Prompt**: "Merchants selling colorful fabrics and spices"

- **Action Prompt**: "A noblewoman inspecting a painting"

Combined Description: "A bustling Italian marketplace during the Renaissance, with artists sketching in the square, merchants selling colorful fabrics and spices, and a noblewoman inspecting a painting."

Example 3: Emotional Portrait

Emotional Tone:

- **Emotion**: Joy

- **Setting Prompt**: "A sunlit meadow"

- **Character Prompt**: "Children playing and laughing"

- **Atmospheric Detail Prompt**: "Bright wildflowers swaying in the breeze"

- **Action Prompt**: "A child flying a kite high in the sky"

Combined Description: "A sunlit meadow with children playing and laughing, bright wildflowers swaying in the breeze, and a child flying a kite high in the sky."

Weight Ratios (:: Notation)

Weight ratios, often denoted by the :: notation, are an advanced technique in prompt writing for AI-generated images. This method allows you to assign different weights to various components of a prompt, thereby influencing the AI's focus and prioritization when generating the image. By adjusting these weight ratios, you can fine-tune the importance of specific elements, achieving more balanced and nuanced results. This section explores the concept of weight ratios, their benefits, and provides practical examples to illustrate their application.

Understanding Weight Ratios (:: Notation)

The ':::' notation is used to specify the relative importance of different elements in a prompt. Each element is assigned a numerical weight, which determines its influence on the final image. The higher the weight, the more emphasis the AI places on that element. This technique is particularly useful for complex prompts where multiple elements need to be balanced to create a coherent and aesthetically pleasing image.

Benefits of Using Weight Ratios

1. **Enhanced Control**:

   o   Weight ratios provide greater control over the AI's interpretation of the prompt, allowing you to fine-tune the balance between different elements.

2. **Improved Focus**:

   o   By assigning higher weights to key elements, you can ensure that the most important aspects of the prompt are prominently featured in the generated image.

3. **Balanced Composition**:

   o   Adjusting weight ratios helps achieve a harmonious composition, ensuring that no single element overwhelms the others.

4. **Customization**:

   o   This technique allows for customized outputs that align closely with specific creative goals and preferences.

Practical Examples of Weight Ratios

Example 1: Creating a Balanced Nature Scene

Prompt:

- "A serene lake::2 with tall pine trees::1 and a small wooden pier::0.5"

Analysis:

- The lake is given the highest weight (2), making it the focal point of the image.

- The pine trees have a moderate weight (1), ensuring they are present but not dominant.

- The wooden pier has the lowest weight (0.5), adding detail without overshadowing the main elements.

Example 2: Depicting a Fantasy Character

Prompt:

- "A fierce dragon::2 with glowing eyes::1.5 and sharp claws::1 in a mystical forest::0.5"

Analysis:

- The dragon is the primary focus with the highest weight (2).

- The glowing eyes are emphasized with a significant weight (1.5), adding intensity to the character.

- The sharp claws are included with a moderate weight (1), providing detail.

- The mystical forest has the lowest weight (0.5), serving as a background that supports the main subject.

Example 3: Illustrating an Urban Scene

Prompt:

- "A bustling street market::1.5 with colorful stalls::1 and diverse crowd::2 under festive decorations::0.5"

Analysis:

The diverse crowd is the main focus with the highest weight (2), ensuring the scene feels lively and populated.

The street market and colorful stalls have weights of 1.5 and 1, respectively, providing context and vibrancy.

The festive decorations have the lowest weight (0.5), adding atmosphere without distracting from the main elements.

Tips for Effective Use of Weight Ratios

1. **Identify Key Elements**:

   o   Determine the most important components of your scene and assign higher weights to these elements.

2. **Maintain Proportionality**:

   o   Ensure that the weights are proportional to the desired emphasis. Avoid extreme disparities unless a dramatic focus shift is required.

3. **Experiment and Adjust**:

   o   Experiment with different weight combinations to see how they affect the output. Adjust as necessary to achieve the desired balance.

4. **Use Contextually**:

   o   Consider the overall context and composition when assigning weights. Ensure that the weights complement each other to create a coherent image.

Advanced Techniques with Weight Ratios

Combining Weight Ratios with Multi-Prompts

Combining weight ratios with multi-prompt techniques can further enhance the complexity and richness of AI-generated images.

Example:

- **Setting Prompt**: "A futuristic cityscape::2"

- **Technology Detail Prompt**: "Hovering vehicles::1.5"

- **Atmospheric Detail Prompt**: "Neon lights::1"

- **Background Prompt**: "Distant mountains::0.5"

Combined Description: "A futuristic cityscape::2 with hovering vehicles::1.5, neon lights::1, and distant mountains::0.5."

Analysis:

- The cityscape is the dominant feature with the highest weight (2).

- Hovering vehicles and neon lights are important details with significant weights (1.5 and 1).

- Distant mountains have the lowest weight (0.5), adding depth without distracting from the main elements.

Weight ratios (:: notation) are a powerful tool for fine-tuning the balance and focus of AI-generated images. By assigning different weights to various elements of a prompt, you can control the emphasis and ensure a harmonious composition. This technique enhances your creative control, allowing for more customized and nuanced outputs. Combining weight ratios with other advanced techniques, such as multi-prompts, further enriches the creative possibilities and helps achieve specific artistic goals more effectively. Experimenting with weight ratios and iterating based on the results will lead to increasingly sophisticated and visually compelling images.

Remix Mode

Remix mode is an advanced technique in prompt writing for AI-generated images that allows you to experiment with and blend various styles, themes, and elements to create unique and innovative outputs. This mode leverages the AI's ability to reinterpret and combine prompts in creative ways, producing results that are distinct from standard prompt usage. This section explores the concept of remix mode, its benefits, and provides practical examples to illustrate how it can be effectively applied.

Understanding Remix Mode

Remix mode involves reimagining and combining different prompts or elements to create a new, cohesive image. This can include merging different styles, themes, or settings, and encouraging the AI to generate creative and unexpected combinations. The goal is to push the boundaries of traditional prompt writing and explore new creative possibilities.

Benefits of Using Remix Mode

1. **Enhanced Creativity**:

   o Remix mode stimulates the AI to think outside the box, leading to innovative and unique image outputs that might not be achievable through conventional prompts.

2. **Versatility**:

   o This technique allows for the blending of diverse themes, styles, and elements, making it highly versatile for various creative projects.

3. **Exploration of New Ideas**:

   o Remix mode encourages experimentation and the exploration of new ideas, helping you discover fresh perspectives and artistic directions.

4. **Dynamic Compositions**:

o By merging different elements, remix mode can create dynamic and visually engaging compositions that capture multiple aspects of a concept.

Practical Examples of Remix Mode

Example 1: Merging Historical and Futuristic Themes

Initial Prompts:

- "A medieval castle"

- "A futuristic cityscape"

Remixed Prompt:

- "A medieval castle integrated with futuristic technology, with knights in shining armor and hover vehicles"

Analysis:

- This remix combines elements of historical and futuristic themes, creating a unique and imaginative setting where past and future coexist.

Example 2: Blending Natural and Urban Environments

Initial Prompts:

- "A lush rainforest"

- "A bustling metropolis"

Remixed Prompt:

- "A bustling metropolis intertwined with lush rainforest elements, with skyscrapers covered in vines and wildlife roaming the streets"

Analysis:

- The remix blends natural and urban elements, resulting in a vibrant and dynamic scene that showcases the harmony between nature and modern architecture.

Example 3: Combining Artistic Styles

Initial Prompts:

- "A surrealist painting"

- "A traditional Japanese garden"

Remixed Prompt:

- "A traditional Japanese garden depicted in a surrealist style, with floating lanterns and abstract, dreamlike features"

Analysis:

This remix merges different artistic styles, creating an image that is both culturally rich and artistically innovative.

Example 4: Fusing Fantasy and Reality

Initial Prompts:

- "A fairytale forest"

- "A contemporary city park"

Remixed Prompt:

- "A contemporary city park transformed into a fairytale forest, with enchanted trees and magical creatures mingling with park visitors"

Analysis:

- The remix fuses fantasy and reality, resulting in a whimsical scene where elements of a fairytale forest are integrated into a modern urban park.

Tips for Effective Use of Remix Mode

1. **Identify Key Elements**:

o Select the main elements or themes you want to blend and ensure they are clearly defined in the prompts.

2. **Encourage Creativity**:

o Use descriptive and evocative language to inspire the AI to think creatively and explore new combinations.

3. **Experiment with Different Combinations**:

o Try various combinations of themes, styles, and settings to see what unique outputs you can achieve.

4. **Iterate and Refine**:

o Continuously iterate and refine your prompts based on the generated images, adjusting as necessary to enhance the final output.

Remix mode is a powerful and versatile technique for enhancing creativity in AI-generated images. By merging different styles, themes, and elements, you can create unique and dynamic compositions that push the boundaries of traditional prompt writing. This approach encourages experimentation and the exploration of new ideas, leading to innovative and visually engaging outputs. Experimenting with remix mode allows for greater creative flexibility and helps achieve specific artistic goals more effectively.

Incorporating Colors and Styles

Incorporating specific colors and styles into your prompts can greatly enhance the visual appeal and coherence of AI-generated images. By guiding the AI with detailed descriptions of color palettes and stylistic directions, you can achieve more targeted and aesthetically pleasing results.

Benefits of Incorporating Colors and Styles

1. **Enhanced Visual Appeal**:

o   Specific colors and styles can make images more visually engaging and attractive.

2. **Cohesive Aesthetic**:

o   Consistent use of colors and styles ensures that all elements of the image work together harmoniously.

3. **Targeted Creativity**:

o   Guiding the AI with specific color schemes and stylistic choices can lead to more precise and creative outputs.

4. **Emotional and Thematic Consistency**:

o   Colors and styles can convey particular emotions and themes, adding depth and meaning to the images.

Techniques for Incorporating Colors

1. **Specify Color Palettes**:

o   Clearly describe the desired color palette to guide the AI in creating images with a consistent and appealing color scheme.

Example:

- **Prompt**: "A serene beach scene with a pastel color palette, featuring soft pinks, blues, and greens"

Analysis:

- This prompt specifies a pastel color palette, guiding the AI to use soft and calming colors, enhancing the serene atmosphere.

2. **Highlight Dominant Colors**:

o Emphasize the dominant colors that should stand out in the image, ensuring that key elements are visually prominent.

Example:

- **Prompt**: "A vibrant marketplace dominated by bright reds and yellows, with splashes of blue and green"

Analysis:

- The prompt highlights dominant colors (reds and yellows) while allowing for secondary colors (blue and green), creating a lively and colorful scene.

3. **Use Color Descriptors**:

o Incorporate descriptive terms for colors to add nuance and specificity to the prompt.

Example:

- **Prompt**: "An enchanted forest with emerald green foliage and golden sunlight filtering through the trees"

Analysis:

- Using descriptive color terms like "emerald green" and "golden sunlight" adds richness and specificity, enhancing the visual detail of the image.

Techniques for Incorporating Styles

1. **Define Artistic Styles**:

o Specify the desired artistic style to guide the AI in generating images with a particular aesthetic.

Example:

- **Prompt**: "A cityscape in the style of Art Deco, with geometric shapes and bold, symmetrical patterns"

Analysis:

- The prompt defines the Art Deco style, guiding the AI to create images with geometric designs and bold patterns typical of this aesthetic.

2. **Combine Multiple Styles**:

o Blend different artistic styles to create unique and innovative images.

Example:

- **Prompt**: "A portrait combining elements of surrealism and impressionism, with dreamlike features and soft, fluid brushstrokes"

Analysis:

- The prompt blends surrealism and impressionism, encouraging the AI to explore creative combinations of these styles.

3. **Incorporate Cultural Styles**:

o Use cultural references to guide the AI in creating images with specific cultural aesthetics.

Example:

- **Prompt**: "A traditional Japanese garden depicted in the Ukiyo-e style, with delicate lines and vibrant colors"

Analysis:

- The prompt references the Ukiyo-e style, guiding the AI to create images with the distinct features of this Japanese art form.

Practical Examples of Incorporating Colors and Styles

Example 1: Landscape Scene

Prompt:

- "A sunset over a tranquil lake, with a warm color palette of oranges, pinks, and purples, in the style of a watercolor painting"

Analysis:

- The prompt specifies a warm color palette and watercolor style, ensuring the image has a soft, serene atmosphere with fluid, blended colors.

Example 2: Fantasy Character

Prompt:

- "A majestic dragon with shimmering emerald scales and fiery red eyes, in the style of high fantasy art, with intricate details and dramatic lighting"

Analysis:

- The prompt highlights specific colors (emerald and red) and the high fantasy style, guiding the AI to create a detailed and visually striking image.

Example 3: Urban Scene

Prompt:

- "A bustling city street at night, illuminated by neon lights in shades of blue and purple, in a cyberpunk style with futuristic elements and dark undertones"

Analysis:

- The prompt defines a color scheme (blue and purple) and a cyberpunk style, leading to a visually dynamic and futuristic urban scene.

Incorporating specific colors and styles into prompts is an advanced technique that enhances the visual appeal, coherence, and creativity of AI-generated images. By specifying color palettes, highlighting dominant colors, and defining artistic styles, you can guide the AI to produce more targeted and aesthetically pleasing outputs. Experimenting with different combinations of colors and styles allows for greater creative flexibility, helping you achieve specific artistic and thematic goals more effectively.

Conclusion

Advanced techniques in prompt writing, such as context layering, thematic consistency, emotional tone, stylistic direction, and symbolism, can significantly enhance the quality, depth, and creativity of AI-generated images. By breaking down complex scenes into simpler components and using detailed, descriptive language, you can guide the AI to produce more nuanced, contextually rich, and visually compelling images. Experimenting with these advanced techniques allows for greater creative flexibility and helps achieve specific artistic and emotional goals more effectively.

Chapter 11: Case Studies and Practical Examples

Understanding advanced prompt writing techniques through case studies and practical examples can provide valuable insights into how these methods can be applied effectively.

Case Study 1: Creating a Complex Urban Scene

Objective:

To create a vibrant and detailed urban scene using weight ratios and multi-prompt techniques.

Initial Prompts:

1. "A busy street at night"

2. "Neon signs and street lights"

3. "Crowds of people walking"

Refined Prompts with Weight Ratios:

1. "A busy street at night::2"

2. "Neon signs and street lights::1.5"

3. "Crowds of people walking::1"

Combined Prompt: "A busy street at night::2, with neon signs and street lights::1.5, and crowds of people walking::1."

Analysis:

*   The busy street is the primary focus, emphasized by the highest weight (2).

*   Neon signs and street lights are important but secondary elements, with a weight of 1.5.

- Crowds of people are included to add liveliness but are less prominent with a weight of 1.

Outcome:

- The generated image showcases a vibrant urban scene with a clear focus on the bustling street, enhanced by the glow of neon lights and the presence of a dynamic crowd.

Case Study 2: Blending Historical and Futuristic Elements

Objective:

To create a scene that blends historical and futuristic elements using remix mode.

Initial Prompts:

1. "A medieval castle"

2. "A futuristic cityscape"

Remixed Prompt:

"A medieval castle integrated with futuristic technology, with knights in shining armor and hover vehicles."

Analysis:

- The prompt merges historical and futuristic themes, creating a unique and imaginative setting.

- The combination encourages the AI to explore creative blends of old and new, resulting in a distinctive visual experience.

Outcome:

- The generated image presents a scene where medieval architecture coexists with advanced technology, showcasing knights alongside hover vehicles, and blending past and future seamlessly.

Case Study 3: Using Colors and Styles in a Fantasy Landscape

Objective:

To create a fantasy landscape with a specific color palette and artistic style.

Initial Prompts:

1. "A mystical forest"

2. "Glowing plants and creatures"

3. "A crystal-clear stream"

Refined Prompts with Colors and Styles:

1. "A mystical forest with a twilight color palette of purples and blues"

2. "Glowing plants and creatures with bioluminescent colors"

3. "A crystal-clear stream reflecting the twilight hues, in the style of an oil painting"

Combined Prompt: "A mystical forest with a twilight color palette of purples and blues, glowing plants and creatures with bioluminescent colors, and a crystal-clear stream reflecting the twilight hues, in the style of an oil painting."

Analysis:

- The twilight color palette creates a magical and serene atmosphere.

- Bioluminescent colors add a fantastical element, enhancing the otherworldly feel.

- The oil painting style gives the image a rich, textured appearance, making it visually captivating.

Outcome:

- The generated image depicts a mystical forest bathed in twilight colors, with glowing flora and fauna, and a stream that mirrors the enchanting hues, all rendered in a beautiful oil painting style.

Practical Example: Creating a Themed Illustration

Objective:

To create an illustration that conveys a theme of transformation using symbolism and metaphor.

Initial Prompts:

1. "A butterfly emerging from a chrysalis"

2. "Morning light filtering through the leaves"

3. "The butterfly spreading its wings for the first time"

Combined Prompt with Symbolism: "A butterfly emerging from a chrysalis, with morning light filtering through the leaves, and the butterfly spreading its wings for the first time, symbolizing transformation and new beginnings."

Analysis:

- The butterfly and chrysalis symbolize transformation and growth.

- Morning light enhances the theme of new beginnings.

- The detailed description ensures that the AI captures the symbolic elements effectively.

Outcome:

- The generated image portrays a butterfly emerging into the morning light, with a sense of renewal and transformation, enriched by the symbolic elements.

Real-World Examples of Effective Prompts

Effective prompt writing can significantly enhance the quality and creativity of AI-generated images. This section presents real-world examples of effective prompts, illustrating how advanced techniques such as specificity, descriptive language, multi-prompting, and contextual layering can be applied to achieve exceptional results.

Example 1: Creating a Detailed Historical Scene

Objective:

To generate a detailed image of an ancient Roman marketplace.

Effective Prompt:

"A bustling Roman marketplace at midday, with merchants selling spices, fruits, and textiles from vibrant stalls. Citizens in togas and tunics barter for goods, while children play near a fountain adorned with statues. The sun casts a warm glow, highlighting the marble columns and terracotta rooftops."

Analysis:

- **Specificity**: The prompt provides specific details about the time of day, types of goods, and clothing, ensuring an accurate historical representation.

- **Descriptive Language**: Vivid descriptions such as "vibrant stalls," "warm glow," and "marble columns" create a rich and immersive scene.

- **Contextual Layering**: The inclusion of merchants, citizens, and children adds layers of activity and context, making the scene dynamic and engaging.

Outcome:

- The generated image is likely to capture the bustling atmosphere of a Roman marketplace, with detailed and historically accurate elements.

Example 2: Depicting a Fantasy Landscape

Objective:

To create an image of a magical forest with mythical creatures.

Effective Prompt:

"A mystical forest bathed in twilight, with towering trees whose leaves glow faintly. Ethereal creatures like fairies and unicorns wander amidst the foliage. A sparkling brook winds through the forest, reflecting the purple and blue hues of the sky. In the distance, an ancient stone archway covered in ivy hints at hidden secrets."

Analysis:

- **Specificity**: The prompt details specific features like "towering trees," "glowing leaves," and "sparkling brook," providing clear visual cues.

- **Descriptive Language**: Terms like "ethereal creatures," "twilight," and "ancient stone archway" enhance the magical and mystical quality of the scene.

- **Contextual Layering**: The inclusion of mythical creatures and an ancient archway adds depth and narrative potential, making the image more intriguing.

Outcome:

- The generated image will likely depict a vibrant and enchanting fantasy landscape, rich in detail and atmosphere.

Example 3: Illustrating a Sci-Fi Environment

Objective:

To create an image of a futuristic cityscape.

Effective Prompt:

"A sprawling futuristic city under a night sky, with sleek skyscrapers made of glass and steel. Neon lights in shades of blue and purple illuminate the streets below, where hover cars zip through the air. Citizens in high-tech attire walk along elevated walkways, and robotic vendors offer a variety of goods. In the center, a towering spire with a rotating holographic display stands as the city's centerpiece."

Analysis:

- **Specificity**: The prompt specifies the architecture, lighting, and activities, ensuring a cohesive futuristic theme.

- **Descriptive Language**: Phrases like "sleek skyscrapers," "neon lights," and "hover cars" create a vivid and dynamic scene.

- **Contextual Layering**: The inclusion of citizens, robotic vendors, and a central spire adds context and complexity, making the city feel alive and futuristic.

Outcome:

- The generated image is expected to be a detailed and immersive depiction of a futuristic city, with a strong emphasis on technology and modernity.

Example 4: Capturing an Emotional Moment

Objective:

To depict a scene that conveys a sense of hope and renewal.

Effective Prompt:

"A solitary figure standing on a cliff at dawn, gazing out at the horizon where the first light of day breaks through the clouds. Wildflowers bloom around the figure's feet, and a gentle breeze rustles their hair. The sky is painted in hues of pink, orange, and gold, symbolizing a new beginning."

Analysis:

- **Specificity**: The prompt provides clear details about the setting, time of day, and emotional tone.

- **Descriptive Language**: Words like "solitary figure," "first light of day," and "hues of pink, orange, and gold" evoke a sense of hope and renewal.

- **Contextual Layering**: The inclusion of wildflowers and a gentle breeze adds sensory details that enhance the emotional impact of the scene.

Outcome:

- The generated image will likely capture the serene and hopeful atmosphere of a new beginning, with a strong emotional resonance.

These real-world examples demonstrate the effectiveness of advanced prompt writing techniques in creating detailed, engaging, and visually compelling AI-generated images. By using specificity, descriptive language, multi-prompting, and contextual layering, you can guide the AI to produce high-quality images that meet specific creative objectives. Experimenting with different approaches and refining your prompts based on the results will help you achieve increasingly sophisticated and impactful images.

Analysis of Successful and Unsuccessful Prompts

Analyzing successful and unsuccessful prompts is crucial for understanding what makes a prompt effective in generating high-quality AI images. By examining both well-crafted and poorly executed prompts, we can identify key elements that contribute to or detract from the desired outcomes.

Analysis of Successful Prompts

Example 1: Creating a Detailed Historical Scene

Successful Prompt: "A bustling Roman marketplace at midday, with merchants selling spices, fruits, and textiles from vibrant stalls. Citizens in togas and tunics barter for goods, while children play near a fountain adorned with statues. The sun casts a warm glow, highlighting the marble columns and terracotta rooftops."

Analysis:

- **Specificity**: The prompt provides specific details about the setting, time of day, and activities, ensuring a clear and accurate representation of a Roman marketplace.

- **Descriptive Language**: Vivid descriptions such as "vibrant stalls," "warm glow," and "marble columns" create a rich, immersive scene.

- **Contextual Layering**: The inclusion of various elements like merchants, citizens, children, and architectural details adds depth and dynamism to the scene.

Outcome:

- The generated image is likely to capture the lively atmosphere of a Roman marketplace with detailed and historically accurate elements.

Key Factors:

- Clear and specific descriptions

- Rich, evocative language

- Multiple layers of context

Analysis of Unsuccessful Prompts

Example 2: Depicting a Fantasy Landscape

Unsuccessful Prompt: "A forest with some trees and magical creatures."

Analysis:

- **Vagueness**: The prompt is too vague, lacking specific details about the forest, the types of trees, and the magical creatures.

- **Lack of Descriptive Language**: The use of generic terms like "some trees" and "magical creatures" fails to create a vivid and engaging image.

- **Insufficient Context**: The prompt does not provide enough context or details to guide the AI in generating a rich and immersive fantasy landscape.

Outcome:

- The generated image is likely to be generic and uninspired, lacking the richness and detail expected in a fantasy landscape.

Key Issues:

- Lack of specificity and detail

- Absence of evocative language

- Insufficient contextual information

Comparative Analysis

Successful Prompt: "A mystical forest bathed in twilight, with towering trees whose leaves glow faintly. Ethereal creatures like fairies and unicorns wander amidst the foliage. A sparkling brook winds through the forest, reflecting the purple and blue hues of the sky. In the distance, an ancient stone archway covered in ivy hints at hidden secrets."

Unsuccessful Prompt: "A forest with some trees and magical creatures."

Comparative Analysis:

- **Specificity**: The successful prompt provides specific details about the time of day (twilight), types of trees (towering with glowing leaves), and the magical creatures (fairies and unicorns), while the unsuccessful prompt is vague and general.

- **Descriptive Language**: The successful prompt uses rich, descriptive language ("bathed in twilight," "ethereal creatures," "sparkling brook") to create a vivid and immersive scene, whereas the unsuccessful prompt lacks such language.

- **Contextual Layering**: The successful prompt includes multiple layers of context, such as the presence of an ancient stone archway and the color reflections in the brook, adding depth and intrigue. The unsuccessful prompt fails to provide additional context or details.

Practical Examples of Prompt Refinement

Example 3: Illustrating a Sci-Fi Environment

Initial Unsuccessful Prompt: "A futuristic city."

Analysis:

- **Vagueness**: The prompt is too vague, providing no specific details about the city's features or elements.

Refined Successful Prompt: "A sprawling futuristic city under a night sky, with sleek skyscrapers made of glass and steel. Neon lights in shades of blue and purple illuminate the streets below, where hover cars zip through the air. Citizens in high-tech attire walk along elevated walkways, and robotic vendors offer a variety of goods. In the center, a towering spire with a rotating holographic display stands as the city's centerpiece."

Analysis:

- **Specificity**: The refined prompt details the city's architecture (sleek skyscrapers), lighting (neon lights in blue and purple), transportation (hover cars), and other elements (robotic vendors, holographic display).

- **Descriptive Language**: The use of vivid terms like "sleek," "illuminate," and "rotating holographic display" creates a dynamic and engaging scene.

- **Contextual Layering**: The inclusion of citizens, vendors, and a central spire adds depth and context, making the city feel alive and futuristic.

Analyzing successful and unsuccessful prompts highlights the importance of specificity, descriptive language, and contextual layering in creating high-quality AI-generated images. Successful prompts provide clear, detailed, and evocative descriptions, guiding the AI to produce rich and immersive scenes. In contrast, unsuccessful prompts often suffer from vagueness, lack of detail, and insufficient context. By refining prompts and incorporating advanced techniques, you can significantly enhance the effectiveness and creativity of your AI-generated images.

Lessons Learned from Case Studies

Analyzing case studies in prompt writing for AI-generated images reveals valuable lessons on crafting effective prompts. By examining both successful and unsuccessful prompts, we can understand the key factors that contribute to high-quality and creative outputs. This section synthesizes the lessons learned from various case studies, providing actionable insights and practical examples.

Lesson 1: Specificity Enhances Clarity and Quality

Example:

- **Unsuccessful Prompt**: "A city park"

- **Successful Prompt**: "A city park in spring, with blooming cherry blossom trees, people picnicking on the grass, and children flying kites under a clear blue sky"

Analysis:

- **Specificity**: The successful prompt provides detailed information about the season (spring), the elements (cherry blossom trees, people picnicking, children flying kites), and the weather (clear blue sky). This specificity guides the AI to create a clear, vivid, and accurate image.

- **Lesson**: Providing specific details about the scene's elements, time, and conditions significantly improves the clarity and quality of the generated image.

Lesson 2: Descriptive Language Creates Rich Imagery

Example:

- **Unsuccessful Prompt**: "A garden"

- **Successful Prompt**: "A lush, tranquil garden with vibrant flowers, a gentle stream, and butterflies fluttering among the blooms"

Analysis:

- **Descriptive Language**: The successful prompt uses vivid adjectives and verbs ("lush," "tranquil," "vibrant," "fluttering") to create a rich and immersive scene.

- **Lesson**: Using descriptive language enhances the visual richness and emotional impact of the generated images, making them more engaging and lifelike.

Lesson 3: Contextual Layering Adds Depth and Complexity

Example:

- **Unsuccessful Prompt**: "A beach"

- **Successful Prompt**: "A serene beach at sunset, with gentle waves lapping the shore, seashells scattered across the sand, and a couple walking hand in hand"

Analysis:

- **Contextual Layering**: The successful prompt includes multiple layers of context: the time of day (sunset), the sensory details (gentle waves, seashells), and human activity (a couple walking). These layers add depth and complexity to the scene.

- **Lesson**: Incorporating various contextual elements creates a more dynamic and engaging image, capturing the viewer's interest and providing a richer narrative.

Lesson 4: Emotional Tone Guides the Atmosphere

Example:

- **Unsuccessful Prompt**: "A person standing on a hill"

- **Successful Prompt**: "A lone traveler standing on a hill at dawn, gazing at the horizon with a sense of hope and anticipation as the first light of day breaks through the clouds"

Analysis:

- **Emotional Tone**: The successful prompt conveys a specific emotional tone ("hope and anticipation") and uses descriptive elements ("first light of day," "breaks through the clouds") to enhance this atmosphere.

- **Lesson**: Defining the emotional tone helps guide the AI to create images that evoke specific feelings and moods, making the scene more impactful.

Lesson 5: Thematic Consistency Ensures Coherence

Example:

- **Unsuccessful Prompt**: "A knight and a dragon"

- **Successful Prompt**: "A brave knight in shining armor faces a fearsome dragon in a dark, enchanted forest, with the moon casting an eerie glow on the scene"

Analysis:

- **Thematic Consistency**: The successful prompt maintains a consistent theme (medieval fantasy) and atmosphere (dark, enchanted), ensuring all elements fit together coherently.

- **Lesson**: Ensuring thematic consistency across all elements of the prompt helps create a harmonious and cohesive image, enhancing the overall visual and narrative appeal.

Practical Application of Lessons Learned

Example 1: Creating a Detailed Urban Scene

Initial Prompt: "A city street"

Refined Prompt: "A bustling city street at dusk, with neon signs illuminating the shops, people hurrying along the sidewalks, and the aroma of street food filling the air"

Lessons Applied:

- **Specificity**: Details about the time of day (dusk), lighting (neon signs), activities (people hurrying), and sensory experiences (aroma of street food).

- **Descriptive Language**: Vivid terms like "bustling," "illuminating," and "filling the air" create a rich scene.

- **Contextual Layering**: Multiple elements and sensory details add depth.

Outcome:

- The refined prompt guides the AI to create a vibrant and dynamic urban scene, rich in detail and atmosphere.

Example 2: Depicting a Fantasy Landscape

Initial Prompt: "A magical forest"

Refined Prompt: "A magical forest at twilight, with bioluminescent plants casting a soft glow, mystical creatures peeking from behind trees, and an ancient stone path leading to a hidden waterfall"

Lessons Applied:

- **Specificity**: Detailed descriptions of the time (twilight), lighting (bioluminescent plants), and specific elements (mystical creatures, ancient stone path).

- **Descriptive Language**: Evocative terms like "bioluminescent," "soft glow," and "hidden waterfall" create a vivid image.

- **Contextual Layering**: Various elements and activities enhance the scene's complexity.

Outcome:

- The refined prompt produces an enchanting and detailed fantasy landscape, capturing the magical atmosphere effectively.

Analyzing case studies of successful and unsuccessful prompts reveals key lessons in effective prompt writing. Specificity, descriptive language, contextual layering, emotional tone, and thematic consistency are essential elements that significantly enhance the quality and creativity of AI-generated images. By applying these lessons, you can refine your prompts to achieve more detailed, engaging, and visually compelling results. Experimentation and iterative refinement based on these principles will lead to increasingly sophisticated and impactful images.

Conclusion

Case studies and practical examples demonstrate the effective application of advanced prompt writing techniques. By utilizing weight ratios, remix mode, and incorporating specific colors and styles, you can create detailed, nuanced, and visually compelling AI-generated images. These examples highlight the importance of refining prompts, experimenting with different combinations, and leveraging advanced techniques to achieve specific creative goals. Through iterative refinement and creative exploration, you can unlock the full potential of AI in generating high-quality and innovative images.

Chapter 12: Troubleshooting Common Issues

Even with careful planning and detailed prompt writing, issues can arise when generating AI images. Understanding common problems and knowing how to troubleshoot them can help you refine your prompts for better results.

Issue 1: Vague or Generic Outputs

Problem: The generated image lacks detail and specificity, resulting in a generic or uninspired output.

Example:

- **Unsuccessful Prompt**: "A beautiful landscape"

Solution: Add specific details and descriptive language to enrich the prompt.

Refined Prompt: "A beautiful landscape with rolling green hills, a sparkling river winding through the valley, and a vibrant sunset painting the sky in shades of orange and pink"

Analysis:

- **Specificity**: Detailed elements like "rolling green hills," "sparkling river," and "vibrant sunset" add depth and clarity.

- **Descriptive Language**: Vivid terms like "sparkling" and "vibrant" enhance the visual appeal.

Issue 2: Inconsistent or Jumbled Elements

Problem: The AI generates an image where elements do not fit together well or appear jumbled and inconsistent.

Example:

- **Unsuccessful Prompt**: "A cityscape with mountains and a beach"

Solution: Clarify the relationship between different elements and ensure thematic consistency.

Refined Prompt: "A modern cityscape at the base of majestic mountains, with a pristine beach along the coastline, where the mountains meet the sea"

Analysis:

- **Clarification**: Specifying the relationship ("at the base of," "along the coastline") helps the AI understand how the elements fit together.

- **Thematic Consistency**: Ensuring all elements belong to a coherent theme (modern cityscape with natural surroundings).

Issue 3: Overcrowded or Cluttered Images

Problem: The image appears too busy or cluttered, making it difficult to focus on any single element.

Example:

- **Unsuccessful Prompt**: "A garden with flowers, trees, fountains, statues, birds, butterflies, and benches"

Solution: Prioritize key elements and reduce the number of details.

Refined Prompt: "A serene garden with blooming flowers and a central fountain, where butterflies flutter around and birds perch on tree branches"

Analysis:

- **Prioritization**: Focusing on fewer key elements ("flowers," "fountain," "butterflies," "birds") creates a cleaner and more focused image.

- **Clarity**: Simplifying the scene helps the AI generate a more coherent and visually pleasing image.

Issue 4: Misinterpretation of the Prompt

Problem: The AI misinterprets the prompt, leading to an image that does not match the intended concept.

Example:

- **Unsuccessful Prompt**: "A bright star in the sky"

Solution: Provide additional context and clarification to guide the AI.

Refined Prompt: "A bright star shining in a clear night sky, surrounded by twinkling constellations and a glowing moon"

Analysis:

- **Context**: Adding details about the night sky and surrounding elements helps the AI understand the intended setting.

- **Clarification**: Ensuring the prompt specifies the context of the star ("clear night sky," "twinkling constellations").

Issue 5: Lack of Emotional Impact

Problem: The generated image lacks the desired emotional tone or fails to evoke the intended feelings.

Example:

- **Unsuccessful Prompt**: "A sad scene"

Solution: Use descriptive language and specific scenarios to convey the emotional tone.

Refined Prompt: "A lone figure standing in the rain, looking down at the ground with a somber expression, as dark clouds gather overhead and raindrops blur the city lights"

Analysis:

- **Descriptive Language**: Using terms like "lone figure," "somber expression," and "dark clouds" effectively conveys sadness.

- **Specific Scenarios**: Describing a specific scenario (standing in the rain, blurred city lights) enhances the emotional impact.

<u>**Common Problems and How to Fix Them**</u>

Crafting effective prompts for AI-generated images can be challenging. Common problems such as vague outputs, inconsistent elements, overcrowded images, misinterpretations, and lack of emotional impact often arise. Understanding these issues and knowing how to fix them can significantly enhance the quality of the generated images.

Common Problems and Solutions

Problem 1: Vague or Generic Outputs

Issue: The generated image lacks detail and specificity, resulting in a generic or uninspired output.

Example:

- **Unsuccessful Prompt**: "A beautiful landscape"

Solution: Add specific details and descriptive language to enrich the prompt.

Refined Prompt: "A beautiful landscape with rolling green hills, a sparkling river winding through the valley, and a vibrant sunset painting the sky in shades of orange and pink"

Analysis:

- **Specificity**: Details about the hills, river, and sunset create a more vivid and specific image.

- **Descriptive Language**: Words like "rolling," "sparkling," and "vibrant" enhance the visual appeal.

Problem 2: Inconsistent or Jumbled Elements

Issue: The AI generates an image where elements do not fit together well or appear jumbled and inconsistent.

Example:

- **Unsuccessful Prompt**: "A cityscape with mountains and a beach"

Solution: Clarify the relationship between different elements and ensure thematic consistency.

Refined Prompt: "A modern cityscape at the base of majestic mountains, with a pristine beach along the coastline, where the mountains meet the sea"

Analysis:

- **Clarification**: Specifying the relationship between the cityscape, mountains, and beach helps the AI understand how the elements fit together.

- **Thematic Consistency**: Ensuring all elements belong to a coherent theme creates a harmonious image.

Problem 3: Overcrowded or Cluttered Images

Issue: The image appears too busy or cluttered, making it difficult to focus on any single element.

Example:

- **Unsuccessful Prompt**: "A garden with flowers, trees, fountains, statues, birds, butterflies, and benches"

Solution: Prioritize key elements and reduce the number of details.

Refined Prompt: "A serene garden with blooming flowers and a central fountain, where butterflies flutter around and birds perch on tree branches"

Analysis:

- **Prioritization**: Focusing on fewer key elements creates a cleaner and more focused image.

- **Clarity**: Simplifying the scene helps the AI generate a more coherent and visually pleasing image.

Problem 4: Misinterpretation of the Prompt

Issue: The AI misinterprets the prompt, leading to an image that does not match the intended concept.

Example:

- **Unsuccessful Prompt**: "A bright star in the sky"

Solution: Provide additional context and clarification to guide the AI.

Refined Prompt: "A bright star shining in a clear night sky, surrounded by twinkling constellations and a glowing moon"

Analysis:

- **Context**: Adding details about the night sky and surrounding elements helps the AI understand the intended setting.

- **Clarification**: Ensuring the prompt specifies the context of the star aids in accurate image generation.

Problem 5: Lack of Emotional Impact

Issue: The generated image lacks the desired emotional tone or fails to evoke the intended feelings.

Example:

- **Unsuccessful Prompt**: "A sad scene"

Solution: Use descriptive language and specific scenarios to convey the emotional tone.

Refined Prompt: "A lone figure standing in the rain, looking down at the ground with a somber expression, as dark clouds gather overhead and raindrops blur the city lights"

Analysis:

- **Descriptive Language**: Words like "lone figure," "somber expression," and "dark clouds" effectively convey sadness.

- **Specific Scenarios**: Describing a specific scenario enhances the emotional impact.

Understanding and addressing common problems in prompt writing is crucial for generating high-quality AI images. By adding specificity, ensuring thematic consistency, reducing clutter, providing context, and enhancing emotional impact, you can significantly improve the effectiveness of your prompts. Continuous experimentation and refinement based on these principles will lead to better results and a deeper understanding of how to craft successful prompts.

<u>Understanding and Resolving Misinterpretations</u>

Misinterpretations in AI-generated images occur when the AI fails to grasp the intended concept or incorrectly interprets the elements of the prompt. This can lead to outputs that do not match the user's expectations. Understanding why misinterpretations happen and learning how to resolve them is crucial for effective prompt writing.

Common Causes of Misinterpretations

1. **Ambiguous Language**:

o   Vague or unclear terms can lead to multiple interpretations, causing the AI to generate unintended results.

2. **Lack of Context**:

o   Without sufficient context, the AI may not understand the relationships between elements, leading to incoherent images.

3. **Overly Complex Prompts**:

o   Complicated prompts with too many elements can confuse the AI, resulting in jumbled or inconsistent images.

4. **Cultural and Contextual Differences**:

o   AI models trained on diverse datasets may misinterpret prompts due to cultural or contextual differences.

Solutions to Misinterpretations

1. **Use Clear and Specific Language**:

o   Ensure that each element of the prompt is described clearly and specifically to reduce ambiguity.

2. **Provide Adequate Context**:

o   Add contextual information to help the AI understand how different elements relate to each other.

3. **Simplify Complex Prompts**:

o   Break down complex prompts into simpler, more manageable parts, and use multi-prompt techniques if necessary.

4. **Consider Cultural and Contextual Nuances**:

o   Be aware of potential cultural and contextual differences and adjust prompts accordingly to ensure accurate interpretations.

Practical Examples

Example 1: Ambiguous Language

Unsuccessful Prompt: "A star on the horizon"

Analysis:

*   The term "star" can refer to both a celestial body and a famous person, leading to potential misinterpretation.

Solution: Clarify the intended meaning by providing additional context.

Refined Prompt: "A bright celestial star on the horizon, shining over the ocean at dusk"

Analysis:

*   The refined prompt specifies "celestial star" and provides context ("shining over the ocean at dusk"), reducing ambiguity.

Outcome:

*   The AI generates an image of a celestial star on the horizon, avoiding any confusion with a famous person.

Example 2: Lack of Context

Unsuccessful Prompt: "A cat on a table"

Analysis:

- Without context, the AI might generate a generic image that lacks detail and interest.

Solution: Provide additional context to enhance the scene.

Refined Prompt: "A fluffy white cat sitting on a wooden dining table, surrounded by potted plants and a bowl of fresh fruit"

Analysis:

- The refined prompt adds specific details about the cat, table, and surroundings, providing a richer context.

Outcome:

- The AI generates a detailed and engaging image of a cat on a table with specific surroundings.

Example 3: Overly Complex Prompts

Unsuccessful Prompt: "A busy street with people walking, cars driving, shops selling various items, street performers entertaining, and a festival taking place"

Analysis:

- The prompt includes too many elements, which can confuse the AI and result in a cluttered image.

Solution: Simplify the prompt and focus on key elements.

Refined Prompt: "A busy street during a festival, with people walking and street performers entertaining the crowd"

Analysis:

- The refined prompt focuses on the festival and street performers, simplifying the scene while maintaining the festive atmosphere.

Outcome:

- The AI generates a more coherent and focused image of a busy street during a festival.

Example 4: Cultural and Contextual Differences

Unsuccessful Prompt: "A traditional wedding"

Analysis:

- The term "traditional wedding" can vary significantly across cultures, leading to diverse interpretations.

Solution: Specify the cultural context to guide the AI accurately.

Refined Prompt: "A traditional Indian wedding with colorful saris, intricate henna designs, and a decorated mandap"

Analysis:

- The refined prompt specifies "Indian wedding" and includes cultural elements like "saris," "henna designs," and "mandap," providing clear context.

Outcome:

- The AI generates an image accurately reflecting the traditional Indian wedding.

Understanding and resolving misinterpretations in AI-generated images involves using clear and specific language, providing adequate context, simplifying complex prompts, and considering cultural and contextual nuances. By addressing these common issues, you can guide the AI to produce more accurate and visually compelling images that match your intended vision. Continuous refinement and iteration based on these principles will lead to increasingly effective prompt writing.

<u>Tips for Consistent Results</u>

Achieving consistent results in AI-generated images can be challenging due to the inherent variability in AI outputs. However, by following certain best practices and employing specific techniques, you can significantly improve the consistency and reliability of your results.

Tips for Consistent Results

1. **Use Specific and Detailed Prompts**

o   Providing clear, specific, and detailed prompts reduces ambiguity and helps the AI understand exactly what you want.

Example:

- **Generic Prompt**: "A garden"

- **Specific Prompt**: "A lush garden with blooming roses, a stone pathway, and a white picket fence"

Analysis:

- The specific prompt provides clear details about the garden's elements, guiding the AI to produce a more accurate and consistent image.

2. **Maintain Consistent Style and Tone**

o   Consistency in the style and tone of your prompts helps the AI generate images that match your desired aesthetic.

Example:

- **Inconsistent Style**: "A modern kitchen" and "A rustic living room"

- **Consistent Style**: "A modern kitchen with sleek appliances" and "A modern living room with minimalist furniture"

Analysis:

- Using a consistent style (modern) across prompts ensures the generated images align aesthetically.

3. **Repeat Key Phrases and Elements**

o Repeating key phrases and elements across prompts reinforces important aspects and helps the AI maintain focus on these elements.

Example:

- **Initial Prompt**: "A serene beach with golden sand"

- **Follow-Up Prompt**: "A serene beach with golden sand and turquoise water"

Analysis:

- Repeating "serene beach with golden sand" in both prompts ensures these elements remain consistent in the generated images.

4. **Use Weight Ratios for Emphasis**

o Applying weight ratios allows you to prioritize certain elements over others, ensuring key aspects of the prompt are consistently emphasized.

Example:

- **Initial Prompt**: "A bustling marketplace"

- **Weighted Prompt**: "A bustling marketplace::2 with colorful stalls::1.5 and street performers::1"

Analysis:

- Assigning higher weights to "bustling marketplace" ensures this element is the primary focus in the image.

5. **Iterate and Refine Prompts**

- Iterative refinement helps you progressively improve the quality and consistency of your prompts based on the generated results.

Example:

- **Initial Prompt**: "A forest with animals"

- **Iteration 1**: "A dense forest with deer and rabbits"

- **Iteration 2**: "A dense forest with tall pine trees, deer grazing, and rabbits hopping through the underbrush"

Analysis:

- Each iteration adds more detail and refines the focus, leading to more consistent and detailed images.

6. **Use Contextual Layering**

- Providing context and layering elements helps the AI understand the relationships between different aspects of the scene.

Example:

- **Initial Prompt**: "A busy street"

- **Contextual Prompt**: "A busy street in a vibrant city, with people walking, cars driving, and shops lining the sidewalks"

Analysis:

- Adding context about the city and street activities helps the AI generate a more coherent and realistic scene.

7. **Leverage Multi-Prompt Techniques**

o Using multiple prompts to describe different aspects of the scene ensures that each element is well-defined and contributes to the overall image.

Example:

- **Single Prompt**: "A futuristic city"

- **Multi-Prompt**:

o **Prompt 1**: "A futuristic city with towering skyscrapers"

o **Prompt 2**: "Neon lights illuminating the streets"

o **Prompt 3**: "Hover cars zipping through the air"

Analysis:

- Breaking down the description into multiple prompts ensures each element is accurately represented and contributes to a consistent image.

Achieving consistent results in AI-generated images requires careful prompt crafting, attention to detail, and iterative refinement. By using specific and detailed prompts, maintaining a consistent style and tone, repeating key phrases, applying weight ratios, iterating and refining, using contextual layering, and leveraging multi-prompt techniques, you can significantly enhance the consistency and quality of your AI-generated images. Continuous experimentation and adjustment based on the generated results will lead to more reliable and visually compelling outputs.

Conclusion

Troubleshooting common issues in prompt writing involves adding specificity, ensuring thematic consistency, reducing clutter, providing context, and enhancing emotional impact. By refining prompts and applying these strategies, you can significantly improve the quality and effectiveness of AI-generated images. Continuous experimentation and iteration will lead to better results and a deeper understanding of how to craft successful prompts.

Chapter 13: Future Trends in AI Art Generation

The field of AI art generation is rapidly evolving, driven by advancements in technology, computational power, and creative methodologies. Future trends in this domain are expected to expand the possibilities for both artists and technologists, offering new tools, techniques, and applications.

Trend 1: Improved Realism and Detail

Development

Advancements in AI algorithms, particularly in generative adversarial networks (GANs) and deep learning, are expected to enhance the realism and detail of AI-generated art. These improvements will allow for the creation of images that are virtually indistinguishable from those produced by human artists.

Example

- **Current Capability**: GANs can generate highly realistic images of human faces, often used in projects like NVIDIA's StyleGAN.

- **Future Enhancement**: Future GAN iterations will likely produce not only realistic faces but also complex scenes with intricate details and textures, such as urban landscapes or detailed natural environments.

Trend 2: Cross-Disciplinary Art Forms

Development

AI art generation is poised to cross traditional boundaries, integrating with other art forms such as music, literature, and performance art. This interdisciplinary approach will create richer and more immersive experiences.

Example

- **Current Capability**: AI tools like OpenAI's MuseNet can compose music in various styles, while GPT-3 can generate textual content.

- **Future Enhancement**: Combining AI-generated music, visual art, and narrative elements could result in multimedia installations or interactive experiences where each element influences the others dynamically.

Trend 3: Personalized Art Creation

Development

AI will increasingly enable personalized art creation, where algorithms generate custom art based on individual preferences, behaviors, and interactions. This trend will leverage user data to tailor art experiences uniquely suited to each person.

Example

- **Current Capability**: Platforms like DeepArt and ArtBreeder allow users to blend and modify images to suit their tastes.

- **Future Enhancement**: AI systems could analyze a user's digital footprint, preferences, and emotional responses to generate personalized art pieces that resonate on a deeper emotional level.

Trend 4: Collaborative AI-Human Art

Development

Collaboration between AI and human artists is expected to become more seamless and sophisticated. AI tools will act as co-creators, assisting artists in the creative process rather than replacing them.

Example

- **Current Capability**: Artists currently use tools like Adobe's Sensei to enhance their creative workflows.

- **Future Enhancement**: AI could suggest creative directions, provide real-time feedback, and adapt its suggestions based on the artist's evolving style, leading to a more dynamic and interactive creative process.

Trend 5: Ethical and Inclusive AI Art

Development

As AI art becomes more prevalent, ethical considerations and inclusivity will play a significant role. Ensuring that AI-generated art reflects diverse perspectives and avoids biases will be crucial.

Example

- **Current Capability**: Efforts are being made to address biases in AI training datasets.

- **Future Enhancement**: AI tools will be developed with built-in mechanisms to ensure inclusivity and fairness, providing a platform for underrepresented voices and creating art that celebrates cultural diversity.

Trend 6: Interactive and Generative Installations

Development

AI-driven interactive installations that respond to audience interactions in real-time are set to become more sophisticated. These installations will create dynamic art experiences that evolve based on viewer engagement.

Example

- **Current Capability**: Interactive installations like teamLab's digital art exhibitions react to audience movements and interactions.

- **Future Enhancement**: Future installations will use AI to interpret more complex inputs such as emotional responses, gestures, and environmental changes, creating truly immersive and evolving art experiences.

Trend 7: AI in Traditional Art Restoration

Development

AI will play a more significant role in art restoration, helping to analyze, restore, and even recreate lost parts of historical artworks with greater accuracy.

Example

- **Current Capability**: AI has been used in projects like the digital restoration of Rembrandt's works.

- **Future Enhancement**: Advanced AI algorithms could assist in identifying original materials and techniques used in historical artworks, providing more accurate and authentic restorations.

Emerging Technologies and Innovations

The field of AI art generation is rapidly evolving, driven by emerging technologies and innovations. These advancements are expanding the boundaries of what AI can achieve in the realm of art, offering new tools, methodologies, and applications that enhance creativity and artistic expression.

Emerging Technologies

1. **Generative Adversarial Networks (GANs)**

Development: GANs have revolutionized AI art by enabling the generation of highly realistic and complex images. The technology involves two neural networks—the generator and the discriminator—that work in tandem to produce increasingly refined outputs.

Example:

- **StyleGAN**: Developed by NVIDIA, StyleGAN allows for the creation of hyper-realistic images by manipulating various attributes (like hair color, age, and expression) in human faces. Future iterations are expected to further improve image quality and offer more control over generated content.

Impact:

- Enhanced realism and detail in AI-generated art, making it indistinguishable from human-created works.

2. **Neural Style Transfer**

Development: Neural style transfer allows the application of the artistic style of one image to the content of another, blending the two to create unique artworks. This technique uses convolutional neural networks (CNNs) to separate and recombine style and content.

Example:

- **DeepArt**: An AI tool that uses neural style transfer to transform photos into artworks in the style of famous painters like Van Gogh or Picasso.

Impact:

- Allows for the exploration of new artistic styles and the fusion of different visual elements to create innovative art.

3. **Transformers in Art Generation**

Development: Transformers, a type of deep learning model originally designed for natural language processing, are now being adapted for visual art generation. These models excel at understanding context and generating coherent, high-quality outputs.

Example:

- **DALL-E**: Developed by OpenAI, DALL-E uses transformers to generate images from textual descriptions. It can create entirely new objects and scenes that combine elements in novel ways.

Impact:

- Enables the creation of unique and imaginative artworks based on textual prompts, bridging the gap between language and visual art.

4. **Augmented Reality (AR) and Virtual Reality (VR)**

Development: AR and VR technologies are increasingly being integrated with AI art generation to create immersive and interactive art experiences. These technologies allow users to experience AI-generated art in three-dimensional spaces.

Example:

- **Tilt Brush**: A VR painting application by Google that allows users to create 3D art in a virtual space. Future developments could integrate AI to assist with or enhance the creative process.

Impact:

- Transforms the way art is experienced, making it more interactive and immersive, and opening up new possibilities for artistic expression.

Innovations in AI Art Generation

1. Interactive AI Art Systems

Innovation: AI systems are being developed that can interact with users in real-time, adjusting and responding to input to create collaborative artworks. These systems use machine learning to understand and adapt to user preferences and actions.

Example:

- **Runway ML**: A creative toolkit that allows artists to use machine learning models to generate, manipulate, and explore images in real-time. Users can experiment with different models and settings to create unique artworks.

Impact:

- Encourages greater collaboration between humans and AI, leading to more personalized and engaging art experiences.

2. AI-Enhanced Art Tools

Innovation: Art tools enhanced with AI capabilities provide artists with new functionalities and efficiencies, such as automatic image generation, style suggestions, and real-time corrections.

Example:

- **Adobe Sensei**: An AI and machine learning platform that powers features in Adobe Creative Cloud, such as content-aware fill, which automatically removes and replaces objects in images.

Impact:

- Enhances the creative workflow, allowing artists to focus more on their artistic vision while AI handles routine or complex tasks.

3. Algorithmic Art Curation

Innovation: AI algorithms are being used to curate art collections and exhibitions, analyzing vast amounts of data to identify trends, themes, and patterns in art. This helps curators make informed decisions about what to include in their exhibitions.

Example:

- **Artrendex**: An AI platform that uses machine learning to analyze and curate art collections, helping galleries and museums organize exhibitions based on data-driven insights.

Impact:

- Provides new ways to explore and present art, enhancing the audience's experience and understanding of artistic trends.

4. AI in Art Restoration

Innovation: AI technologies are being developed to assist in the restoration of damaged or deteriorated artworks. These tools can analyze historical data and existing artwork to suggest accurate restoration methods and materials.

Example:

- **REPAIR (Reconstructing Pixels by Attending to Image Regions)**: An AI model that helps restore old paintings by predicting the original colors and textures of missing or damaged parts.

Impact:

- Preserves cultural heritage and allows for more accurate and efficient restoration of valuable artworks.

Emerging technologies and innovations in AI art generation are transforming the landscape of artistic creation and expression.

Advances in GANs, neural style transfer, transformers, AR/VR, interactive systems, AI-enhanced tools, algorithmic curation, and art restoration are expanding the possibilities for both artists and audiences. By embracing these technologies, the future of AI art generation promises to be more creative, immersive, and collaborative, pushing the boundaries of what is possible in the world of art.

The Future of Prompt Writing

The future of prompt writing for AI art generation is poised for significant advancements, driven by the continuous evolution of AI technologies and deeper integration with creative processes. As AI models become more sophisticated, the way we craft prompts will evolve to harness these advancements fully.

Trend 1: Context-Aware Prompt Writing

Development

Future AI systems will increasingly incorporate context-awareness, understanding the broader context of prompts to generate more relevant and coherent images. This involves interpreting the intent behind prompts and considering previous interactions and external factors.

Example

- **Current Capability**: An AI generates an image based solely on the given prompt without considering user history or environmental context.

- **Future Enhancement**: An AI that remembers user preferences and previous prompts to tailor outputs. For example, if a user frequently requests images with a fantasy theme, the AI can incorporate subtle fantasy elements even in unrelated prompts unless instructed otherwise.

Example Prompt:

- **Context-Aware Prompt**: "Create a serene landscape suitable for a fantasy novel cover, considering the previous preferences for lush forests and mystical elements."

Impact:

- Enhanced relevance and personalization of AI-generated images, making the outputs more aligned with the user's overarching goals and preferences.

Trend 2: Multi-Modal Prompt Integration

Development

Multi-modal AI systems will integrate different types of inputs, such as text, voice, images, and gestures, to create more dynamic and interactive art generation experiences. This integration allows for more nuanced and complex prompt inputs.

Example

- **Current Capability**: Text-based prompts are the primary method for guiding AI-generated images.

- **Future Enhancement**: Combining voice commands, sketches, and text to create a comprehensive prompt. For instance, a user might describe a scene verbally, sketch a rough layout, and provide a textual description of specific elements.

Example Prompt:

- **Multi-Modal Prompt**: "Sketch a layout of a city street, describe it verbally as 'a bustling marketplace at dusk,' and provide a text note: 'Include neon lights and street performers.'"

Impact:

- More precise and richer art generation by combining various input methods, allowing for a fuller expression of creative intent.

Trend 3: Interactive and Iterative Prompt Refinement

Development

Interactive and iterative prompt refinement will become a standard feature, allowing users to continuously refine and adjust prompts based on real-time feedback from the AI. This will enable a more collaborative and dynamic creative process.

Example

- **Current Capability**: Users provide a single prompt and wait for the final output without real-time interaction.

- **Future Enhancement**: A conversational interface where users can iteratively refine the image by giving continuous feedback and adjustments. For example, after generating an initial image, a user can request changes like "make the sky darker" or "add more trees to the left side."

Example Prompt:

- **Interactive Prompt**: "Generate an image of a tranquil beach at sunset. (After initial output) Please add a lighthouse on the horizon and make the waves more prominent."

Impact:

- A more flexible and user-driven art generation process, enabling continuous improvement and customization of the final output.

Trend 4: Enhanced Descriptive Language Processing

Development

Advancements in natural language processing (NLP) will allow AI systems to better understand and process complex and nuanced language, resulting in more accurate and detailed image generation from descriptive prompts.

Example

- **Current Capability**: Basic understanding of descriptive language, sometimes missing subtle nuances or complex descriptions.

- **Future Enhancement**: AI systems capable of understanding and accurately interpreting detailed and nuanced descriptions, such as idiomatic expressions, metaphors, and multi-layered narratives.

Example Prompt:

- **Enhanced Descriptive Prompt**: "Create a hauntingly beautiful forest where the trees have an ethereal glow, and the ground is covered in a soft, misty haze that feels both inviting and mysterious."

Impact:

- More sophisticated and accurate image generation, capturing the full depth and nuance of complex descriptive prompts.

Trend 5: AI-Assisted Creativity Tools

Development

AI-assisted creativity tools will become more integrated into the prompt writing process, providing real-time suggestions and enhancements to help users craft better prompts. These tools will leverage AI to suggest improvements, alternative phrasings, and additional details.

Example

- **Current Capability**: Basic text editors with limited AI assistance.

- **Future Enhancement**: Advanced AI-driven creativity assistants that analyze prompts and suggest enhancements. For example, an AI might suggest adding specific atmospheric details or adjusting the prompt structure for better results.

Example Prompt:

- **AI-Assisted Prompt**: "Generate an image of a medieval marketplace." (AI Suggestion: "Consider adding details about the time of day, specific market activities, and the types of goods being sold for a richer scene.")

Impact:

- Improved prompt quality and creativity through AI-assisted enhancements, leading to more detailed and compelling images.

The future of prompt writing for AI art generation is set to become more sophisticated, interactive, and personalized. Context-aware prompts, multi-modal input integration, interactive refinement, enhanced descriptive language processing, and AI-assisted creativity tools are key trends that will shape the next generation of AI art generation. By leveraging these advancements, users will be able to create more nuanced, accurate, and visually stunning AI-generated art, pushing the boundaries of what is possible in digital creativity.

How to Stay Updated and Continue Learning

The field of AI art generation is dynamic and rapidly evolving. Staying updated with the latest trends, technologies, and methodologies is crucial for artists, technologists, and enthusiasts who want to remain at the forefront of this innovative domain.

Engaging with Online Communities

Development: Online communities such as forums, social media groups, and dedicated platforms are vibrant hubs for sharing knowledge, experiences, and the latest developments in AI art.

Examples:

- **Reddit**: Subreddits like r/MachineLearning, r/DeepLearning, and r/AIArt are valuable resources for discussions, news, and tutorials.

- **Discord**: Servers dedicated to AI art, such as the "AI Art Creators" community, offer real-time discussions, collaborations, and feedback from peers.

Benefits:

- Access to a wide range of perspectives and expertise.

- Opportunities for collaboration and networking.

- Real-time updates on the latest trends and technologies.

Attending Conferences and Workshops

Development: Conferences and workshops provide in-depth insights into the latest research, innovations, and applications in AI art generation. These events often feature presentations, panels, and hands-on sessions by leading experts.

Examples:

- **NeurIPS (Conference on Neural Information Processing Systems)**: One of the premier conferences for machine learning and AI, featuring sessions on AI art.

- **AI and Creativity Workshops**: Various workshops focused on the intersection of AI and creative arts, offering practical training and networking opportunities.

Benefits:

- Exposure to cutting-edge research and developments.

- Opportunities to interact with experts and thought leaders.

- Hands-on experience with new tools and techniques.

Following Industry Publications and Blogs

Development: Industry publications, academic journals, and blogs are excellent sources of in-depth articles, research papers, and case studies on AI art generation.

Examples:

- **Medium**: Blogs like "Towards Data Science" and "The Gradient" often feature articles on AI art and machine learning.

- **ArXiv**: A repository of research papers where you can find the latest academic research on AI art generation and related fields.

Benefits:

- Access to detailed and authoritative content.

- Insights into both theoretical and practical aspects of AI art.

- Keeping abreast of the latest research findings and technological advancements.

Enrolling in Online Courses and Tutorials

Development: Online platforms offer a variety of courses and tutorials that cover different aspects of AI art generation, from basic principles to advanced techniques.

Examples:

- **Coursera**: Offers courses like "AI For Everyone" by Andrew Ng and specialized courses on generative models and creative AI.

- **Udacity**: Provides nanodegree programs in AI and deep learning that include modules on generative models and AI art.

Benefits:

- Structured learning paths that cover comprehensive topics.

- Flexibility to learn at your own pace.

- Access to expert instructors and peer support.

Experimenting with AI Tools and Platforms

Development: Practical experimentation with AI art tools and platforms allows you to apply theoretical knowledge and gain hands-on experience.

Examples:

- **Runway ML**: A platform that provides various machine learning models for creative applications, including art generation.

- **DeepArt**: An AI tool that allows users to transform photos into artworks in the style of famous painters.

Benefits:

- Direct experience with AI tools and technologies.

- Opportunities to create and refine your own AI-generated art.

- Understanding the practical challenges and limitations of AI art generation.

Reading Books and Academic Papers

Development: Books and academic papers provide deep insights into the theories, methodologies, and historical context of AI art generation.

Examples:

- **Books**: Titles like "The Creativity Code" by Marcus du Sautoy explore the intersection of AI and creativity.

- **Academic Papers**: Reading papers from conferences like CVPR (Conference on Computer Vision and Pattern Recognition) and journals like IEEE Transactions on Neural Networks and Learning Systems.

Benefits:

- Comprehensive understanding of foundational theories and advanced concepts.

- Exposure to diverse perspectives and research findings.

- Enhancing critical thinking and analytical skills.

Engaging with AI Art Projects and Collaborations

Development: Participating in AI art projects and collaborations can provide practical experience and expose you to innovative approaches and ideas.

Examples:

- **Collaborative Projects**: Joining projects on platforms like GitHub where developers and artists collaborate on AI art tools and applications.

- **Artist Residencies**: Programs that offer residencies for artists working with AI, providing resources, mentorship, and a collaborative environment.

Benefits:

- Practical experience in applying AI to art.

- Opportunities to work with and learn from other creatives.

- Exposure to real-world challenges and innovative solutions.

Staying updated and continuing to learn in the rapidly evolving field of AI art generation requires a proactive and multi-faceted approach. Engaging with online communities, attending conferences and workshops, following industry publications, enrolling in online courses, experimenting with AI tools, reading books and academic papers, and participating in collaborative projects are all effective strategies. By leveraging these resources and opportunities, you can stay at the forefront of AI art generation, continuously enhancing your knowledge and skills in this exciting and innovative domain.

Conclusion

The future of AI art generation is filled with exciting possibilities, driven by continuous advancements in technology and a deeper understanding of artistic processes. Improved realism, cross-disciplinary integration, personalized creation, collaborative efforts, ethical considerations, interactive installations, and art restoration are some of the key trends that will shape the future of this field. Embracing these trends will not only enhance the capabilities of AI art but also expand the horizons of human creativity.

Conclusion

AI art generation stands at the intersection of technology and creativity, offering unprecedented opportunities for artists and technologists alike. As we've explored throughout this comprehensive guide, the advancements in AI technologies, the evolution of prompt writing, and the emerging trends in the field are reshaping the landscape of artistic creation.

Recap of Key Points

1. **Advanced Techniques**:

- **Weight Ratios**: Using the :: notation to emphasize specific elements in prompts enhances the focus and quality of the generated images. For example, specifying "A bustling marketplace::2 with colorful stalls::1.5 and street performers::1" ensures that the marketplace is the central focus.

- **Remix Mode**: This technique blends various styles and themes to create unique and innovative outputs. Combining prompts like "A medieval castle" with "A futuristic cityscape" results in a scene where historical architecture meets advanced technology.

2. **Emerging Technologies**:

- **GANs and Neural Networks**: These technologies continue to push the boundaries of realism and detail in AI-generated art. The development of StyleGAN has shown how finely-tuned attributes can create hyper-realistic human faces and complex scenes.

- **Augmented Reality (AR) and Virtual Reality (VR)**: Integrating AI with AR and VR is transforming the way we experience art, making it more immersive and interactive.

Tools like Google's Tilt Brush are paving the way for future AI-driven creative processes.

3. **Future Trends**:

o **Context-Aware Prompt Writing**: AI systems that understand and remember user preferences will lead to more personalized and relevant art generation. An AI that tailors outputs based on past interactions can create more cohesive and meaningful artworks.

o **Multi-Modal Prompt Integration**: Combining text, voice, sketches, and gestures will allow for richer and more precise prompt inputs, enhancing the creative process.

4. **Staying Updated and Continuing Learning**:

o **Engaging with Online Communities**: Platforms like Reddit and Discord provide valuable resources for staying informed about the latest developments in AI art.

o **Attending Conferences and Workshops**: Events like NeurIPS offer insights into cutting-edge research and innovations.

o **Experimenting with AI Tools**: Hands-on experience with platforms like Runway ML and DeepArt helps solidify theoretical knowledge and fosters practical skills.

Real-World Impact and Future Directions

The integration of AI in art generation is not just about creating visually stunning images; it's about expanding the horizons of human creativity. AI tools and techniques are empowering artists to explore new mediums and methods, fostering collaboration, and democratizing access to sophisticated creative technologies.

For instance, the ability of AI to restore and preserve cultural heritage through projects like REPAIR highlights its practical applications beyond mere artistic creation. Similarly, personalized art creation based on user preferences represents a significant leap towards truly individualized art experiences.

Examples of Transformative Applications

1. **Art Restoration**:

- **REPAIR**: Utilizing AI to predict and restore original colors and textures in historical paintings ensures the preservation of cultural heritage with remarkable accuracy.

2. **Personalized Art**:

- AI systems analyzing user data to generate personalized artworks resonate deeply with individual preferences, offering a unique and personal connection to art.

3. **Interactive Installations**:

- Advanced AI-driven installations that respond to viewer interactions in real-time create dynamic art experiences, transforming passive viewers into active participants.

Encouragement for Continued Experimentation

The field of AI art generation is continually evolving, offering endless opportunities for innovation and creativity. As we've explored, advanced techniques, emerging technologies, and the future trends in AI art generation provide a rich landscape for experimentation. Embracing this spirit of innovation is crucial for anyone looking to push the boundaries of what AI and art can achieve together.

The Power of Experimentation

Experimentation is at the heart of creativity. By continuously experimenting with new tools, techniques, and ideas, you can discover unique artistic expressions and novel applications of AI. Here are a few ways to foster a culture of experimentation in AI art generation:

1. **Try New Tools and Technologies**:

o Don't be afraid to explore new AI tools and platforms. For example, experimenting with platforms like Runway ML, DeepArt, or Google's DeepDream can provide fresh perspectives and capabilities.

o Example: Using **Runway ML**, you might combine StyleGAN with other models to create hybrid images that blend realism and surrealism in unprecedented ways.

2. **Iterate and Refine**:

o Continuous iteration and refinement of your prompts and techniques are essential. Start with a basic idea and gradually add layers of detail and complexity.

o Example: Begin with a prompt like "A serene beach at sunset" and iteratively refine it by specifying elements such as "gentle waves," "palm trees swaying," and "soft orange glow of the setting sun."

3. **Explore Cross-Disciplinary Approaches**:

o Combine AI art with other art forms or fields to create interdisciplinary works. This could involve integrating music, literature, or even scientific concepts into your visual art.

o   Example: Create an interactive installation that combines AI-generated visual art with AI-composed music, reacting to viewer movements or environmental changes in real-time.

4. **Collaborate with Others**:

o   Collaboration can spark new ideas and lead to innovative outcomes. Work with other artists, technologists, and AI experts to explore different perspectives and skill sets.

o   Example: Partner with a writer to generate AI art based on descriptive passages from their stories, creating a visual narrative that complements the text.

Real-World Examples of Experimentation

1. **AI-Generated Portraits**:

o   Artists have used AI to create portraits that blend historical styles with modern elements. For instance, experimenting with GANs to produce portraits that mimic the brushstrokes of Van Gogh but feature contemporary subjects.

2. **Dynamic and Interactive Art**:

o   Projects like teamLab's interactive installations, where AI art responds to audience interaction, showcase the potential of combining technology with human engagement. Experiment with sensors and interactive technology to create art that changes based on viewer input.

3. **Augmented Reality Art**:

o   Use AR to overlay AI-generated art onto real-world environments. Experiment with AR platforms to create immersive art experiences that blend the digital and physical worlds.

Encouraging a Culture of Experimentation

To foster a culture of experimentation, consider the following:

- **Stay Curious and Open-Minded**: Always be on the lookout for new ideas and be willing to step out of your comfort zone.

- **Learn from Failures**: Not every experiment will be successful, but each failure provides valuable insights. Use these experiences to refine your approach.

- **Document Your Process**: Keep a record of your experiments, including what worked and what didn't. This documentation can be a valuable resource for future projects and for sharing your learnings with others.

- **Share and Collaborate**: Engage with the AI art community by sharing your work and collaborating on projects. Platforms like GitHub, art forums, and social media are excellent places to connect with others and get feedback.

The journey of AI art generation is one of continuous exploration and innovation. By embracing experimentation, leveraging new technologies, and fostering collaboration, you can unlock new creative potentials and contribute to the evolving landscape of AI art. Whether you are an artist, technologist, or enthusiast, staying curious, open-minded, and proactive in your learning and experimentation will ensure that you remain at the cutting edge of this exciting field.

Final Thoughts

The fusion of artificial intelligence and art marks a transformative era in creative expression. AI art generation is not just a technological advancement; it represents a profound shift in how we conceive, create, and experience art. This convergence opens up endless possibilities, allowing artists and technologists to collaborate in unprecedented ways and pushing the boundaries of creativity.

Reflecting on the Journey

Throughout this comprehensive exploration of AI art generation, we've delved into the intricacies of advanced techniques, emerging technologies, and future trends. We've examined how AI tools like GANs, neural networks, and transformers are revolutionizing the creation of art, enabling artists to achieve new levels of detail, realism, and innovation. The integration of AI with AR and VR is transforming the art experience, making it more immersive and interactive.

Examples:

- **StyleGAN**: This tool has demonstrated how AI can generate hyper-realistic images by manipulating attributes like facial expressions and hair color, pushing the boundaries of portrait creation.

- **Runway ML**: This platform empowers artists to experiment with various AI models, allowing for real-time creative exploration and iteration.

Embracing Continuous Learning and Experimentation

The future of AI art generation is a dynamic landscape that requires continuous learning and experimentation. By staying engaged with online communities, attending conferences, following industry publications, and experimenting with new tools, you can stay at the forefront of this evolving field.

Examples:

- **Online Communities**: Platforms like Reddit and Discord offer valuable resources and real-time discussions that keep you updated on the latest developments.

- **Conferences**: Events like NeurIPS provide insights into cutting-edge research and innovations, fostering a deeper understanding of AI technologies.

Encouragement for Future Endeavors

The most significant takeaway is the importance of embracing a mindset of innovation and curiosity. Whether you are an artist looking to incorporate AI into your creative process or a technologist exploring the artistic potential of AI, the key is to remain open to new ideas and continually push the boundaries of what is possible.

Example:

- **Interactive Installations**: Projects like teamLab's exhibitions demonstrate how AI can create dynamic, interactive art that responds to audience input, transforming the viewer into an active participant in the creative process.

Final Thoughts

AI art generation is more than a technological novelty; it is a new frontier in the artistic landscape. By integrating AI into the creative process, we can explore uncharted territories of imagination and innovation. This journey requires a commitment to continuous learning, collaboration, and experimentation. As we move forward, the fusion of human creativity and artificial intelligence promises to redefine the boundaries of art, offering new opportunities for expression and connection.

Embrace this transformative potential, stay curious, and continue to experiment. The future of art is not just in the hands of artists or technologists alone but in the collaborative spirit that bridges these worlds. Together, we can create a richer, more vibrant tapestry of human creativity enhanced by the power of AI.

Conclusion

The future of AI art generation is bright and filled with potential. By embracing advanced techniques, leveraging emerging technologies, and staying committed to continuous learning, artists and technologists can unlock new realms of creativity and innovation. The journey ahead promises not only to redefine artistic boundaries but also to enrich the human experience through the fusion of art and artificial intelligence. As we move forward, the collaboration between human creativity and AI will undoubtedly lead to new, unforeseen possibilities, making the world of art more vibrant and inclusive than ever before.

Appendices

Appendices provide supplementary information that supports the main content of a book or report. They include detailed data, additional resources, and practical examples that enhance the reader's understanding.

Structure of Appendices

1. **Appendix A: Technical Terms and Definitions**

2. **Appendix B: Sample Prompts and Outputs**

3. **Appendix C: Tools and Platforms for AI Art Generation**

4. **Appendix D: Research Papers and Further Reading**

5. **Appendix E: Tutorials and Workshops**

Appendix A: Technical Terms and Definitions

Purpose: To clarify technical jargon and concepts used throughout the book.

Example:

- **Generative Adversarial Network (GAN)**: A class of machine learning frameworks where two neural networks, the generator and the discriminator, compete with each other to improve the accuracy of the generated outputs.

- **Neural Style Transfer**: A technique that applies the artistic style of one image to the content of another using convolutional neural networks.

Usage: Refer to this appendix whenever a technical term is introduced to ensure readers understand the concepts without disrupting the flow of the main text.

Appendix B: Sample Prompts and Outputs

Purpose: To provide concrete examples of prompts and the resulting AI-generated images, illustrating the practical application of concepts discussed in the book.

Example:

1. **Prompt**: "A serene beach at sunset with golden sands and gentle waves."

   o **Output**: [Insert image of a beach at sunset with described elements]

2. **Prompt**: "A bustling futuristic city with neon lights and flying cars."

   o **Output**: [Insert image of a futuristic cityscape]

Usage: Use these examples as a reference to understand how specific prompts translate into visual outputs, helping to refine prompt-writing skills.

Appendix C: Tools and Platforms for AI Art Generation

Purpose: To list and describe various tools and platforms available for AI art generation, including their features and use cases.

Example:

- **Runway ML**: A platform that offers an array of machine learning models for creative applications, including image generation, style transfer, and video processing.

- **DeepArt**: An online tool that uses neural style transfer to transform photos into artworks in the style of famous painters.

Usage: Refer to this appendix to explore different tools and platforms, helping to choose the right one for specific creative needs.

Appendix D: Research Papers and Further Reading

Purpose: To provide a curated list of academic papers, articles, and books that offer deeper insights into AI art generation.

Example:

- **"Image Style Transfer Using Convolutional Neural Networks"** by Gatys et al.: A foundational paper on neural style transfer.

- **"A Style-Based Generator Architecture for Generative Adversarial Networks"** by Karras et al.: A key paper on the development of StyleGAN.

Usage: Use this appendix to delve deeper into the theoretical underpinnings of AI art generation and stay updated with the latest research developments.

Appendix E: Tutorials and Workshops

Purpose: To list practical resources such as online tutorials, workshops, and courses that provide hands-on experience with AI art tools and techniques.

Example:

- **Coursera**: Offers courses like "AI For Everyone" by Andrew Ng and specialized courses on generative models.

- **Udacity**: Provides nanodegree programs in AI and deep learning, including modules on generative models and creative AI.

Usage: Refer to this appendix to find resources for further learning and skill development, enhancing practical knowledge in AI art generation.

Glossary of Terms

The glossary of terms is a valuable resource that provides clear and concise definitions of technical jargon and concepts used throughout the book.

Glossary of Terms

A

Adversarial Training: A machine learning technique where two models are trained simultaneously, such as in GANs, with one generating data and the other evaluating it to improve performance iteratively.

Algorithm: A set of rules or instructions given to an AI to help it learn and make decisions. In the context of AI art generation, algorithms define how the AI processes inputs and produces outputs.

B

Backpropagation: A method used in neural networks to calculate the gradient of the loss function with respect to each weight by the chain rule, allowing the network to update weights and learn from errors.

Bias: In AI, bias refers to the systematic errors that can arise from the training data or the design of the model, which can lead to unfair or inaccurate outcomes. It's important to minimize bias to ensure fair AI-generated art.

C

Convolutional Neural Network (CNN): A class of deep neural networks commonly used for analyzing visual imagery. CNNs are particularly effective in tasks like image recognition and classification, crucial for AI art generation.

CycleGAN: A type of GAN that learns to translate images from one domain to another without needing paired examples. It's used in applications like style transfer and image-to-image translation.

D

Deep Learning: A subset of machine learning involving neural networks with many layers. Deep learning models are capable of learning from large amounts of data, making them ideal for complex tasks like image generation.

Discriminator: In a GAN, the discriminator is a neural network that evaluates how real or fake an image looks, guiding the generator to produce more realistic outputs.

E

Epoch: One complete pass through the entire training dataset. In the context of AI art generation, multiple epochs are typically required to train a model effectively.

Encoder-Decoder Network: A type of neural network architecture often used in tasks involving transformation from one type of data to another, such as image captioning or translation.

F

Feature Extraction: The process of identifying important characteristics or patterns within input data, which can then be used to generate more accurate outputs in AI models.

Fine-Tuning: The process of taking a pre-trained model and making slight adjustments to it to improve performance on a specific task. This is common in AI art generation to adapt a model to new artistic styles.

G

Generative Adversarial Network (GAN): A framework where two neural networks, the generator and the discriminator, are trained together. The generator creates images, and the discriminator evaluates them, improving the quality of the generated images over time.

Gradient Descent: An optimization algorithm used to minimize the loss function in machine learning models by iteratively adjusting the model's parameters.

H

Hyperparameter: Settings or configurations used to structure and train a machine learning model. Examples include learning rate, batch size, and the number of epochs.

Hyperrealism: An art movement characterized by highly realistic and detailed artworks, often achieved through advanced AI techniques in art generation.

I

Inference: The process of using a trained AI model to make predictions or generate outputs based on new input data.

Instance Normalization: A normalization technique used in style transfer models to normalize the output of each instance in a batch independently, helping to maintain style consistency.

J

Joint Attention: In AI art generation, this refers to the ability of the AI to focus on multiple elements of an image or prompt simultaneously, ensuring coherence and detail in the generated output.

Jupyter Notebook: An open-source web application that allows for interactive computing and is commonly used for developing and testing machine learning models.

K

Kernel: In the context of convolutional neural networks, a kernel (or filter) is a small matrix used to apply effects like blurring, sharpening, or edge detection to images.

K-means Clustering: A method of vector quantization used for partitioning data into clusters, which can be used in AI art generation to group similar styles or elements together.

L

Latent Space: An abstract multidimensional space where data is encoded by an AI model. In GANs, the generator maps points from the latent space to realistic images.

Learning Rate: A hyperparameter that controls how much to change the model in response to the estimated error each time the model's weights are updated.

M

Machine Learning (ML): A subset of artificial intelligence that involves the use of algorithms and statistical models to enable computers to perform tasks without explicit instructions.

Mode Collapse: A common problem in GANs where the generator produces a limited variety of outputs, reducing the diversity of generated images.

N

Neural Network: A series of algorithms that mimic the operations of a human brain to recognize patterns and relationships in data. Essential in tasks like image recognition and generation.

Normalization: The process of scaling input data to improve the efficiency and performance of the machine learning model. Techniques include batch normalization and instance normalization.

O

Overfitting: When a machine learning model learns the training data too well, including its noise and outliers, leading to poor generalization to new data.

Optimizer: Algorithms used to adjust the weights of the neural network to minimize the loss function, such as Adam, SGD, and RMSprop.

P

Pre-training: The process of training a model on a large dataset before fine-tuning it on a smaller, more specific dataset. Common in transfer learning approaches.

PyTorch: An open-source machine learning library based on the Torch library, widely used for developing deep learning models.

Q

Quantization: The process of mapping a large set of input values to a smaller set, often used in reducing the precision of the numbers to improve computational efficiency.

Quickdraw Dataset: A dataset of doodles collected by Google that can be used to train AI models in recognizing and generating simple drawings.

R

Reinforcement Learning (RL): A type of machine learning where an agent learns to make decisions by performing actions in an environment to maximize cumulative reward.

Residual Networks (ResNets): A type of neural network that uses skip connections to allow the model to learn residual functions, helping to mitigate the vanishing gradient problem.

S

Semi-Supervised Learning: A type of machine learning that uses a small amount of labeled data and a large amount of unlabeled data for training, improving efficiency and performance.

Style Transfer: The process of applying the artistic style of one image to the content of another using neural networks.

T

TensorFlow: An open-source machine learning library developed by Google, widely used for building and training deep learning models.

Transfer Learning: A machine learning technique where a model developed for one task is reused as the starting point for a model on a second task.

U

Unsupervised Learning: A type of machine learning that involves training a model on data without labeled responses, used for discovering hidden patterns or intrinsic structures.

Upsampling: The process of increasing the resolution of an image or feature map, often used in generative models to produce higher resolution outputs.

V

Variational Autoencoder (VAE): A type of autoencoder that learns to encode data into a latent space distribution, allowing for the generation of new data points.

Vision Transformer (ViT): A type of transformer model adapted for image analysis tasks, offering state-of-the-art performance in image recognition and generation.

W

Weight Initialization: The process of setting the initial weights of a neural network before training begins, which can significantly affect the model's performance and convergence speed.

Word2Vec: A technique for natural language processing that represents words in vector space, capturing their meanings and relationships.

X

XGBoost: An efficient and scalable implementation of gradient boosting framework, commonly used in machine learning competitions and applications for its high performance.

XML (eXtensible Markup Language): A language used to define rules for encoding documents in a format that is both human-readable and machine-readable, often used in data interchange.

Y

YOLO (You Only Look Once): A real-time object detection system that applies a single neural network to the full image, dividing it into regions and predicting bounding boxes and probabilities for each region.

Yelp Dataset: A large dataset containing information about businesses, reviews, and user data, often used in training and testing recommendation systems and sentiment analysis models.

Z

Zero-Shot Learning: A method where a model is trained to recognize objects or concepts without having seen any examples during training, using auxiliary information like semantic attributes.

Z-Score Normalization: A statistical technique used to standardize the values of a dataset by subtracting the mean and dividing by the standard deviation, ensuring a mean of zero and a standard deviation of one.

This glossary of terms provides essential definitions and explanations for the key concepts and terminology used in AI art generation. By familiarizing yourself with these terms, you can deepen your understanding of the subject and more effectively navigate the complexities of AI-driven creative processes. Use this glossary as a reference to clarify technical jargon and enhance your learning experience throughout the book.

Additional Resources and Tools

The field of AI art generation is vast and continually evolving, with a plethora of resources and tools available to artists, technologists, and enthusiasts.

Software and Platforms

1. **Runway ML**

o   **Description**: A creative toolkit that provides access to machine learning models for generating art, video editing, and other creative tasks. It offers a user-friendly interface that allows artists to experiment with AI without deep technical knowledge.

o   **Example Use Case**: Artists can use Runway ML to create surreal images by applying GAN models or to edit videos with real-time style transfer effects.

2.   **DeepArt**

o   **Description**: An online tool that uses neural style transfer to transform photos into artworks in the style of famous painters like Van Gogh or Picasso.

o   **Example Use Case**: Users can upload a photo and select an artistic style to generate a unique artwork that blends their image with the chosen style.

3.   **Google's DeepDream**

o   **Description**: A computer vision program that uses a convolutional neural network to find and enhance patterns in images, creating dream-like, psychedelic visuals.

o   **Example Use Case**: Artists can input an image and adjust the level of abstraction to produce intricate and surreal visuals.

4.   **Artbreeder**

o   **Description**: A collaborative platform that allows users to generate and explore images using GANs. Users can blend images, adjust features, and create new variations through a simple interface.

o   **Example Use Case**: Create new characters by blending features from different faces or generate landscapes by combining various environmental elements.

5. **Adobe Sensei**

o   **Description**: An AI and machine learning platform integrated into Adobe Creative Cloud, enhancing tools like Photoshop and Illustrator with features such as content-aware fill, intelligent upscaling, and auto-tagging.

o   **Example Use Case**: Use content-aware fill to seamlessly remove objects from images or employ intelligent upscaling to enlarge photos without losing quality.

Educational Materials

1. **Coursera**

o   **Courses**: Offers a variety of courses on AI, machine learning, and creative AI. Notable courses include "AI For Everyone" by Andrew Ng and specialized courses on generative models.

o   **Example Use Case**: Enroll in "Generative Adversarial Networks (GANs)" to learn about the theory and practical applications of GANs in art generation.

2. **Udacity**

o   **Nanodegree Programs**: Provides in-depth programs in AI and deep learning, including modules focused on generative models and creative applications.

o   **Example Use Case**: Complete the "Deep Learning Nanodegree" to gain hands-on experience with neural networks and their application in creating art.

3. **Khan Academy**

o **AI and Machine Learning Content**: Offers foundational courses in computer science and AI, suitable for beginners looking to understand the basics.

o **Example Use Case**: Start with "Introduction to Neural Networks" to build a solid foundation before exploring more complex AI art generation techniques.

Community Hubs and Forums

1. **Reddit**

o **Subreddits**: r/MachineLearning, r/DeepLearning, and r/AIArt are active communities where users share news, research, tutorials, and artworks.

o **Example Use Case**: Participate in discussions on r/AIArt to get feedback on your projects and discover new techniques.

2. **Discord**

o **Servers**: Join AI and art-related servers such as "AI Art Creators" to engage in real-time conversations, share work, and collaborate with others.

o **Example Use Case**: Collaborate on a group project using shared resources and real-time feedback from peers.

3. **GitHub**

o **Repositories**: Access open-source projects, code repositories, and collaborative tools for AI art generation. Examples include repositories for StyleGAN, DeepArt, and other popular models.

o **Example Use Case**: Fork a repository of an AI art project to experiment with the code and contribute improvements or new features.

Research Papers and Articles

1. **ArXiv**

   o **Research Papers**: A repository of research papers on AI, machine learning, and computer vision. Topics include neural networks, GANs, and style transfer.

   o **Example Use Case**: Read papers like "Image Style Transfer Using Convolutional Neural Networks" by Gatys et al. to understand the underlying principles of style transfer.

2. **Medium**

   o **Blogs and Articles**: Platforms like "Towards Data Science" and "The Gradient" publish articles on the latest trends and advancements in AI art.

   o **Example Use Case**: Follow authors who specialize in AI art generation to stay updated with new techniques and case studies.

Tutorials and Workshops

1. **YouTube**

   o **Tutorial Channels**: Channels like "Two Minute Papers" and "Sentdex" offer tutorials and explanations on AI and machine learning topics.

   o **Example Use Case**: Watch step-by-step tutorials on implementing GANs or style transfer models to enhance your practical skills.

2. **Online Workshops**

   o **Platforms**: Websites like Eventbrite and Meetup often list workshops and webinars on AI art generation and related technologies.

o **Example Use Case**: Attend a virtual workshop on using AI in creative workflows to gain hands-on experience and network with professionals.

The appendices provide a wealth of additional resources and tools to support your journey in AI art generation. By leveraging software and platforms, educational materials, community hubs, research papers, and tutorials, you can continuously enhance your skills and stay updated with the latest developments in this dynamic field. Use these resources to explore new techniques, collaborate with others, and push the boundaries of your creative potential.

Recommended Reading

Staying informed about the latest developments in AI art generation requires continuous learning and exploration. This section provides a list of recommended readings, including books, articles, and research papers that offer valuable insights into the theoretical foundations, practical applications, and future trends of AI in art. These resources are essential for anyone looking to deepen their understanding and expand their knowledge in this dynamic field.

Books

1. **"The Creativity Code: How AI is Learning to Write, Paint and Think" by Marcus du Sautoy**

o **Description**: This book explores the intersection of artificial intelligence and creativity, examining how AI is being used to create art, literature, and music. Du Sautoy delves into the philosophical and practical implications of AI as a creative tool.

- o **Example**: The book discusses how algorithms can mimic the style of great artists like Rembrandt, and what this means for the future of art.

2. **"Deep Learning" by Ian Goodfellow, Yoshua Bengio, and Aaron Courville**

- o **Description**: A comprehensive textbook on deep learning, covering the theoretical underpinnings and practical applications of neural networks. This book is essential for understanding the core technologies behind AI art generation.

- o **Example**: The chapters on convolutional neural networks and generative models are particularly relevant for those interested in image generation and manipulation.

3. **"Artificial Intelligence: A Guide for Thinking Humans" by Melanie Mitchell**

- o **Description**: Mitchell provides a broad overview of AI, including its history, current capabilities, and future potential. The book is accessible to both technical and non-technical readers.

- o **Example**: The book includes discussions on machine learning, neural networks, and their applications in various fields, including art.

Articles and Papers

1. **"Image Style Transfer Using Convolutional Neural Networks" by Leon A. Gatys, Alexander S. Ecker, and Matthias Bethge**

- o **Description**: This seminal paper introduces a method for transferring the style of one image to the content of another using CNNs. It is foundational for understanding neural style transfer techniques.

o **Example**: The authors demonstrate how their method can create images that combine the content of a photograph with the style of a famous painting.

2. **"A Style-Based Generator Architecture for Generative Adversarial Networks" by Tero Karras, Samuli Laine, and Timo Aila**

o **Description**: This paper presents StyleGAN, a powerful GAN architecture that allows for high-resolution image synthesis with controllable style variations.

o **Example**: The paper includes examples of how StyleGAN can generate photorealistic images of human faces and discusses the architecture's impact on creative AI applications.

3. **"Creative Adversarial Networks (CANs): Generating 'Art' by Learning About Styles and Deviating from Style Norms" by Ahmed Elgammal et al.**

o **Description**: This paper introduces CANs, a type of GAN designed to generate creative and novel artworks by learning and deviating from established artistic styles.

o **Example**: The authors show how CANs can produce artworks that are both novel and stylistically coherent, demonstrating the potential of AI to contribute to the field of art.

Journals and Online Publications

1. **"Journal of Artificial Intelligence Research (JAIR)"**

o **Description**: A peer-reviewed open-access journal that publishes research in all areas of artificial intelligence, including machine learning and its applications in art.

o **Example**: Articles in JAIR cover cutting-edge research and methodologies, providing in-depth insights into the latest advancements in AI.

2. **"Towards Data Science" (Medium Publication)**

o **Description**: An online publication that features articles and tutorials on data science, machine learning, and AI. It includes practical guides and case studies relevant to AI art generation.

o **Example**: Articles on generative adversarial networks, neural style transfer, and AI in creative industries offer practical advice and theoretical knowledge.

3. **"The Gradient" (Medium Publication)**

o **Description**: A publication focused on machine learning research and industry applications. It provides a platform for researchers and practitioners to share their insights and findings.

o **Example**: In-depth articles on the latest research papers, trends, and technological advancements in AI art generation.

Online Courses and Tutorials

1. **"Generative Adversarial Networks (GANs) Specialization" by DeepLearning.AI on Coursera**

o **Description**: A series of courses that provide a comprehensive understanding of GANs, including their architecture, training techniques, and applications in generating art.

o **Example**: The specialization includes hands-on projects where learners can build and train their own GAN models for creative purposes.

2. **"Creative Applications of Deep Learning with TensorFlow" on Udacity**

o **Description**: This course focuses on using TensorFlow to create AI-generated art, music, and literature. It covers both the theoretical concepts and practical implementations.

o **Example**: Learners can experiment with deep learning models to generate artworks and understand the creative potential of AI.

The recommended readings listed in this appendix provide a solid foundation for understanding AI art generation's theoretical and practical aspects. By exploring these books, articles, papers, journals, and online courses, you can deepen your knowledge, stay updated with the latest developments, and enhance your skills in this rapidly evolving field. Use these resources to continue your journey into the fascinating world of AI-generated art, pushing the boundaries of creativity and innovation.

Conclusion

Appendices are essential for providing additional context and resources that complement the main content of a book or report. By including technical terms, sample prompts, tools, research papers, and tutorials, the appendices serve as a valuable reference for readers seeking to deepen their understanding and application of AI art generation. Use these appendices to access detailed information and practical examples that support and enrich your learning journey.

Examples

Prompt "A peaceful meadow, with wildflowers in full bloom and butterflies fluttering around"

Dr. Hesham Mohamed Elsherif

Prompt "A wise old wizard, with a long, flowing beard, holding a staff topped with a glowing crystal."

Prompt " A modern city skyline, with an ancient temple in the foreground "

Dr. Hesham Mohamed Elsherif

Prompt "A serene lake reflecting the colorful autumn foliage, with a majestic mountain range in the background."

Prompt "A vibrant city street at night, with bustling crowds of people, neon lights illuminating the scene, street performers entertaining passersby, and food vendors selling a variety of snacks."

Dr. Hesham Mohamed Elsherif

Prompt "A mystical forest with towering trees, magical creatures roaming the forest, glowing plants illuminating the area, and a crystal-clear stream flowing through the forest."

Prompt "A grand medieval battlefield, with knights in shining armor, horses charging into battle, banners flying in the wind, and a castle standing tall in the background."

Prompt "A tranquil forest glade, with deer grazing peacefully, wildflowers in full bloom, and a sparkling stream flowing gently."

Prompt "A bustling market at dusk, with vendors selling exotic fruits and spices, customers haggling and buying goods, and lanterns and string lights illuminating the stalls."

Dr. Hesham Mohamed Elsherif

Prompt "A mystical battlefield, with knights in shining armor clashing with dragons, enchanted forests and glowing runes in the background, and fire and lightning illuminating the sky."

Prompt "An eerie, mist-covered graveyard with a brooding vampire in a flowing black cloak, bats flying under a crescent moon, and the vampire standing beside an ancient, crumbling tombstone."

Prompt "An elegant skyscraper with geometric designs, luxurious furnishings with bold, symmetrical patterns, a palette of gold, black, and deep green, and soft, ambient lighting highlighting the intricate details."

Prompt "A chrysalis hanging from a branch with a butterfly emerging, morning light filtering through the leaves, and the butterfly spreading its wings for the first time."

Dr. Hesham Mohamed Elsherif

Prompt "A futuristic city on a distant planet with hover cars zipping through neon-lit streets, twin suns setting in the purple sky, and aliens and humans coexisting peacefully."

Prompt "A sunlit meadow with children playing and laughing, bright wildflowers swaying in the breeze, and a child flying a kite high in the sky."

Dr. Hesham Mohamed Elsherif

Prompt "A bustling metropolis intertwined with lush rainforest elements, with skyscrapers covered in vines and wildlife roaming the streets"

Prompt "A traditional Japanese garden depicted in a surrealist style, with floating lanterns and abstract, dreamlike features"

Dr. Hesham Mohamed Elsherif

Prompt "A contemporary city park transformed into a fairytale forest, with enchanted trees and magical creatures mingling with park visitors"

Prompt "A medieval castle integrated with futuristic technology, with knights in shining armor and hover vehicles."

Prompt "A mystical forest with a twilight color palette of purples and blues, glowing plants and creatures with bioluminescent colors, and a crystal-clear stream reflecting the twilight hues, in the style of an oil painting."

Prompt "A butterfly emerging from a chrysalis, with morning light filtering through the leaves, and the butterfly spreading its wings for the first time, symbolizing transformation and new beginnings."

Dr. Hesham Mohamed Elsherif

Prompt "A bustling Roman marketplace at midday, with merchants selling spices, fruits, and textiles from vibrant stalls. Citizens in togas and tunics barter for goods, while children play near a fountain adorned with statues. The sun casts a warm glow, highlighting the marble columns and terracotta rooftops."

Prompt "A sprawling futuristic city under a night sky, with sleek skyscrapers made of glass and steel. Neon lights in shades of blue and purple illuminate the streets below, where hover cars zip through the air. Citizens in high-tech attire walk along elevated walkways, and robotic vendors offer a variety of goods. In the center, a towering spire with a rotating holographic display stands as the city's centerpiece."

Dr. Hesham Mohamed Elsherif

Prompt "A solitary figure standing on a cliff at dawn, gazing out at the horizon where the first light of day breaks through the clouds. Wildflowers bloom around the figure's feet, and a gentle breeze rustles their hair. The sky is painted in hues of pink, orange, and gold, symbolizing a new beginning."

Prompt "A bustling Roman marketplace at midday, with merchants selling spices, fruits, and textiles from vibrant stalls. Citizens in togas and tunics barter for goods, while children play near a fountain adorned with statues. The sun casts a warm glow, highlighting the marble columns and terracotta rooftops."

Prompt "A mystical forest bathed in twilight, with towering trees whose leaves glow faintly. Ethereal creatures like fairies and unicorns wander amidst the foliage. A sparkling brook winds through the forest, reflecting the purple and blue hues of the sky. In the distance, an ancient stone archway covered in ivy hints at hidden secrets."

Prompt "A magical forest at twilight, with bioluminescent plants casting a soft glow, mystical creatures peeking from behind trees, and an ancient stone path leading to a hidden waterfall"

Dr. Hesham Mohamed Elsherif

Prompt "A beautiful landscape with rolling green hills, a sparkling river winding through the valley, and a vibrant sunset painting the sky in shades of orange and pink"

Prompt "A serene garden with blooming flowers and a central fountain, where butterflies flutter around and birds perch on tree branches"

Dr. Hesham Mohamed Elsherif

Prompt "A bright star shining in a clear night sky, surrounded by twinkling constellations and a glowing moon"